COOKING WITH

Bon Appétit

COOKING WITH
Bon Appétit

Soups and
Salads

THE KNAPP PRESS
Publishers
Los Angeles

Published by The Knapp Press
5455 Wilshire Boulevard, Los Angeles, California 90036

Library of Congress Cataloging in Publication Data

Main entry under title:

Cooking with Bon appétit.

    Includes index.
    1. Soups. 2. Salads. I. Bon appétit. II. Title: Soups and salads.
TX757.C66 1983   641.8′13   82-23295
ISBN 0-89535-116-1

On the cover: *Tomato-Vegetable Soup*

Printed and bound in the United States of America

10   9   8   7   6   5   4   3   2

❦ Contents

🍎 Foreword

"Soup or salad?" spoken in a weary voice by a bored waiter, charts the unpromising course of too many restaurant meals. It implies routine: something to keep the customers at bay while the chef concentrates on the important courses.

At *Bon Appétit* we believe that soups and salads can be among the most stimulating aspects of any meal. As first courses they can ready the palate for delights to come. In heartier versions they can serve as the focus for superb, less formal lunches, brunches or dinners. Some can even make refreshing finales for rich repasts. Not the least of their wonders is that most soups and many salads permit, and even benefit from, preparation a day or more in advance.

To enhance your appreciation of these often-ignored courses, we've collected over 200 international recipes from the pages of *Bon Appétit*. Some are as exotic as a Southeast Asian Hot and Sour Soup (page 41) or a Greek-style Roasted Pepper Salad with Feta and Shrimp (page 89). Others are as down-home as Southern-Style Corn Chowder (page 17) and a very special Chef's Salad (page 101). There are cold dessert soups, such as Iced Cantaloupe Soup (page 56), and hot salads, such as Marinated Hot Carrot Salad (page 60). There are simple broths that are perfect for the lightest menu, and hearty stews and main-course salads that will leave everyone sated. Naturally, recipes for a variety of dressings and suggestions for garnishes are included.

For easy menu planning, the six chapters in this volume are arranged by courses in order of appearance: first course, main course and cold soups, appetizer and side-dish salads, main course and fruit salads. Introductions to each chapter offer helpful advice for choosing the appropriate recipes for any occasion, and special features throughout provide professional tips and instructions that range from selecting the proper olive oil (page 83) to making classic mayonaise (pages 90–91) or a fish stock from scratch (pages 36–37).

We heartily recommend every recipe included in this volume. We have tested and tasted them all in our own kitchens, and our readers have praised them. We know they will spur you on to imaginative feats in the kitchen and to new delights at the table. And we feel certain that this remarkable variety of recipes will take the routine out of soups and salads for good and raise them to the level where they belong.

1 ❧ First-Course Soups

First courses inspire almost limitless variety in taste and presentation, offering substantial room for creativity, and making them fun to plan. At the same time, however, they pose a unique challenge. Because they set the stage for the dishes to come, at their best they should both stimulate the cook's imagination and whet the appetite without overwhelming the rest of the meal.

For the busy host or hostess, soups fill both these requirements particularly well. Soup-making need not require any difficult or time-consuming techniques and, in most cases, first-course soups can be made several days ahead and reheated just before serving. And soups offer a seemingly endless range of flavors, textures and consistencies, from a fragrant cup of Four-Mushroom Consommé (page 2), a fresh-tasting vegetable puree like All-Weather Broccoli Soup (page 2) or piquant Chicken and Clam Broth (page 9) to the suave elegance of cream soups such as Herbed Carrot Cream with Peas (page 15), Crab Bisque (page 25) or Pimiento Soup with Vermouth (page 20).

Shimmering stocks, consommés and broths are, of course, the most important ingredients for any good soup, but they are also delicious served alone, as low-calorie but full-flavored starters for lighter suppers. Not only can they be prepared months ahead and frozen, but their usefulness is compounded when they're blended with other ingredients to create more complex—and delectable—combinations. Consider the classic French onion soup: simple chicken broth is transformed into a robust dish through the addition of generous portions of caramelized onions, croutons and cheese. The version on page 5 receives a splash of Calvados and applejack for a delicious twist on an old favorite.

🍎 Vegetable Broths

All-Weather Broccoli Soup

Can also be served cold.
Garnish with plain yogurt.

4 servings

4 cups chopped fresh broccoli
2 cups chicken broth
1 small onion, quartered
1 garlic clove, halved

1 teaspoon fresh lemon juice
Salt and freshly ground pepper
Lemon slices (garnish)

Combine broccoli, broth, onion and garlic in large saucepan over medium-high heat and cook until broccoli is tender, about 10 to 15 minutes. Transfer to blender in batches and puree until smooth. Return to saucepan. Add lemon juice and season with salt and pepper. Cook until heated through. Ladle soup into bowls and garnish with lemon slices.

Four-Mushroom Consommé

8 servings

1 ounce dried Polish or Italian (porcini) mushrooms
1 ounce dried Japanese shiitake mushrooms
6 cups chicken stock
1 pound mushrooms, stems minced and caps sliced
3 tablespoons minced shallot
1 teaspoon salt
¼ teaspoon freshly ground pepper

2 tablespoons dry Sherry
2 teaspoons soy sauce

3 egg whites
2 eggshells, crumbled

3 cups water
Several drops fresh lemon juice
Uncooked enoki mushrooms or sliced mushroom caps (garnish)

Soak dried mushrooms in stock in large saucepan until soft, about 2 hours. Remove with slotted spoon. Discard any hard stems or pieces, then mince mushrooms. Return to saucepan and add minced mushroom stems (reserve sliced caps), shallot, salt and pepper. Bring to simmer over medium-high heat; reduce heat and let simmer 40 minutes, skimming occasionally and keeping level of liquid constant by adding water. Remove from heat and stir in Sherry and soy sauce.

Beat egg whites with eggshells in 4-quart stainless steel bowl. Whisking constantly, gradually add broth to whites. Return to saucepan, place over medium heat and whisk gently until liquid is simmering. Stop stirring but let *simmer* for 15 minutes (*do not allow to boil*). Egg whites will coagulate and float to top, forming a cap.

Meanwhile, line strainer or sieve with 2 layers of cheesecloth and set over large bowl. Gently ladle consommé into strainer, pressing liquid through cheesecloth with back of ladle. Taste broth and adjust seasoning.

Combine water and lemon juice in small saucepan and bring to boil. Add sliced mushroom caps and parboil 2 minutes. Drain well and transfer to clean saucepan and add strained consommé. Bring to simmer. Ladle into bowls and garnish with uncooked mushrooms.

Chinese Stuffed Cucumber Soup

6 to 8 servings

Filling
1½ ounces dried black mushrooms
¾ pound fresh ground pork
1 tablespoon chopped green onion (white part only)
1 large egg, slightly beaten
½ teaspoon sesame oil
2 teaspoons Sherry
2 teaspoons chopped Chinese parsley (cilantro)

½ teaspoon salt
¼ teaspoon sugar
Pinch of white pepper

3 large cucumbers, peeled, cut into ½-inch lengths and seeded
6 cups boiling chicken stock
Green onion shreds (garnish)
Cilantro (garnish)

Soak mushrooms in boiling water about 30 minutes. Drain well. Chop by hand or in food processor to form a paste. Combine with the remaining filling ingredients.

Stuff generously into cucumber sections. Steam 15 minutes. Place in large serving bowl. Add stock. Garnish with onion shreds and cilantro.

Potato Soup with Vegetable Julienne

Serve hot or chilled.

6 to 8 servings

6 tablespoons vegetable oil (preferably cold-pressed safflower)
5 large potatoes, peeled and sliced
1 large yellow onion, chopped
6 cups (or more) water

2 medium carrots, cut into 1½-inch matchsticks
2 large leeks (white part only), well washed and cut into 1½-inch matchsticks

1 small head Boston lettuce, finely shredded
Herb or vegetable salt

2 egg yolks
3 tablespoons water
¼ cup chopped fresh chervil or parsley

Combine 3 tablespoons oil, potato, onion and water in heavy 4-quart saucepan. Bring to boil over medium-high heat. Reduce heat, cover and simmer until potato is soft, about 10 to 15 minutes. Transfer mixture to processor or blender in batches and puree (or press through fine strainer).

Return puree to saucepan, adding more water if soup is too thick. Place over medium-low heat and simmer 5 minutes. Remove from heat.

Heat remaining oil in medium skillet over low heat. Add carrot, leek and lettuce. Season to taste with herb salt. Cover and cook slowly until vegetables are crisp-tender, about 2 to 3 minutes. Stir vegetables into soup.

Whisk egg yolks with 3 tablespoons water in small mixing bowl. Add about ½ cup hot soup to yolks. Stir yolk mixture into soup. Place over low and heat through; do not boil. Adjust seasoning. To serve, ladle soup into bowls and top with chervil or parsley.

Maui Corn Soup

6 servings

2 tablespoons vegetable oil
½ cup minced onion
1 garlic clove, minced
6 cups chicken broth
2 cups corn kernels
1 teaspoon ground ginger
½ teaspoon sugar

¼ teaspoon freshly ground pepper
2 tablespoons soy sauce
2 tablespoons water
1 tablespoon cornstarch
2 eggs
2 green onions, thinly sliced
Additional soy sauce (garnish)

Heat oil in large saucepan over medium-high heat until hot. Add onion and garlic and sauté 2 minutes. Pour in broth and bring to boil. Stir in corn, ginger, sugar and pepper. Reduce heat to low, cover and cook until heated through, about 7 minutes. Combine soy sauce, water and cornstarch in small bowl. Slowly blend into soup, stirring constantly until thickened. Beat eggs with green onion in small bowl. Gradually add to soup, stirring until eggs are just set. Ladle into bowls and serve immediately. Pass additional soy sauce separately.

Mixed Vegetable Soup

Makes 5 cups

2 tablespoons (¼ stick) butter
½ cup fresh peas (about ½ pound unshelled)
3 ounces green beans, cut into ½-inch pieces
1 small turnip (about 3 ounces), peeled and cut into ½-inch pieces
1 small boiling potato (about 3 ounces), peeled and cut into ½-inch pieces
1 small leek (white part only), cut into ¼-inch slices (about ½ cup sliced)

2 sprigs fresh thyme or ½ teaspoon dried, crumbled
4 cups chicken stock or water
1 medium tomato (about 6 ounces), peeled, seeded, juiced and coarsely chopped
Lemon juice (optional)
Salt and freshly ground pepper
Thickener (optional) (see box, pages 6–7)
Enrichment (optional) (see box, pages 6–7)
4 to 6 tablespoons butter (optional)

Melt 2 tablespoons butter in heavy 2-quart saucepan over low heat. Add peas, beans, turnip, potato, leek and thyme. Cover and cook 10 minutes, stirring occasionally. Add stock, increase heat and bring to boil. Let boil until vegetables are tender, skimming off any foam that rises to surface, about 10 minutes. Stir in tomato. Season with lemon juice, salt and pepper. Thicken and enrich as desired. (If soup is not enriched, place a tablespoon of butter in bottom of each bowl.) Ladle into bowls and serve immediately.

Can be kept warm in top of double boiler or in bain-marie after thickening, but do not add enrichment until just before serving.

Onion Soup with Cheese Crouton

4 to 6 servings

¼ cup (½ stick) butter
4 large yellow onions, thinly sliced
½ teaspoon sugar
6 cups canned beef broth
1 teaspoon Worcestershire sauce
½ teaspoon paprika

Salt and freshly ground pepper

4 to 6 slices French bread
Butter
¼ cup (about) freshly grated
Parmesan or Gruyère cheese

Heat butter in large saucepan over medium heat. Add onion and sugar and sauté until golden. Add broth, Worcestershire and paprika and bring to boil. Reduce heat and simmer uncovered 15 to 20 minutes. Add salt and pepper.

Meanwhile, toast bread on one side under broiler. Spread untoasted side with butter and sprinkle with cheese. Return to broiler until lightly toasted.

Ladle soup into bowls and float toast. *If soup bowls are ovenproof, float bread and run under broiler to toast second side.*

Onion Soup with Calvados

The familiar French onion soup is delightful, but in this lighter broth, you can taste the pure flavor of slowly cooked onion heightened by the addition of a bit of Calvados.

2 servings

2 tablespoons (¼ stick) butter
1 large onion, chopped
Pinch of brown sugar
2 cups chicken broth

¼ teaspoon thyme
1 bay leaf
Salt and freshly ground pepper
½ ounce Calvados or applejack

Melt butter in heavy skillet over low heat. Add onion, sprinkle with sugar and sauté slowly until light caramel color, about 7 to 10 minutes. Add broth, thyme, bay leaf, salt and pepper and blend well. Cover and continue cooking for 20 minutes. Stir in Calvados or applejack just before serving.

Sweet Pea and Zucchini Soup

2 servings

1½ cups rich chicken stock
   (preferably homemade)
1 medium zucchini, cut into ½-inch
   slices
½ cup fresh or frozen tiny peas
   (petits pois)

¼ cup chopped onion
½ teaspoon chervil
1 tablespoon butter
Salt and freshly ground pepper

Combine stock, zucchini, peas, onion and chervil in medium saucepan over medium heat and bring to boil. Reduce heat and simmer until zucchini is tender, about 10 minutes. Transfer to blender and puree until smooth. Return soup to saucepan and warm over low heat. Whisk in butter. Season to taste with salt and pepper.

🍂 *Vegetable Soups*

Heartily satisfying served hot or cold—or hot one night and cold the next—aromatic vegetable soups are honest elixirs that nourish the soul. Chock-full of robust, garden-fresh produce, they provide a showcase for the bounty of each season.

Quickly and easily prepared in advance, they can be served with salad and bread for wholesome budget-stretching lunches or dinners. When they precede other courses, the more costly portions of meat and fish can be decreased. Simple as they are, soups set the tone of a meal: Rich purees and sturdy broths enhance straightforward broiled or poached entrées, while the enriched versions can add a light touch to multicourse dinners.

Generally, vegetable soups can be divided into two categories: the natural, chunkier, nonpureed or the pureed. For nonpureed, use equal amounts of vegetables (no more than five, so the individual character of each will be discernible), cutting them into equal sizes to promote even cooking. Add the hardest vegetables to the stock first and let them cook a bit before adding softer textured ones. That way all the vegetables will be perfectly crisp-tender. Pasta, barley, lentils or precooked dried beans can be a delightful fillip. Try some of these savory combinations: red peppers, green peppers, zucchini and eggplant; tomatoes, summer and winter squash; or cabbage, leeks, turnips, Swiss chard and corn. The fresher the ingredients and finer the stock, the better the result. However, make sure you don't mix a strongly flavored stock with a more delicate vegetable—the broth will overwhelm it.

A pureed soup is simply a blend of one or more cooked vegetables or legumes with enough liquid (usually stock, cream, milk, water or a mixture) to make them spoonable. When using greens or nonstarchy vegetables such as cucumbers or mushrooms, consult our suggestions for thickeners, since one must be added to bind and add body. Firmer vegetables, such as carrots, peas, beans, asparagus, artichoke bottoms, celery root, turnip and broccoli, can be transformed into purees by boiling them until tender, then pureeing them in small batches with a blender or processor, or passing them through the fine disk of a food mill.

These more substantial vegetables create soups that do not need to be thickened, but if you prefer a heartier version, you may wish to do so. You can also use different combinations for interesting variations, such as asparagus and peas; cabbage, brussels sprouts and cauliflower; celery root, potato and turnip; or leeks, turnip, potato and watercress.

Thickeners
Use any of the following. Proportions are for 1 cup of soup.

- *Roux:* Melt 1 tablespoon butter in heavy saucepan over low heat. Add 1 tablespoon flour and stir until mixture is thick and smooth, about 3 to 5 minutes. Add stock gradually and stir until mixture boils. Add cooked vegetables and continue with recipe.

- *Beurre Manié:* Mix 1 tablespoon butter with 1 tablespoon flour. Just before serving, stir into soup a little at a time.

- *Cornstarch, Potato Starch or Arrowroot:* Mix 1½ teaspoons with 1 tablespoon cold water. Just before serving, blend mixture into soup and simmer for 2 minutes without stirring.
- *Rice or Potato:* Cook 1½ tablespoons rice in 2 cups boiling water or cook ⅓ cup minced peeled potato in enough water to cover until tender. If soup is to be pureed, drain rice or potato and combine with other ingredients. If not, drain and puree with some of stock before blending into soup.
- *Farina, Semolina or Tapioca:* Add 1½ teaspoons farina, semolina flour or quick-cooking tapioca to soup after it reaches boiling point.
- *Egg Yolks and Cream:* Beat 1 egg yolk with ¼ cup whipping cream or crème fraîche. Gradually whisk in 1 cup hot soup, then slowly stir this mixture back into remaining soup. Cook over medium heat, stirring constantly, until soup thickens, about 4 to 5 minutes.

Enrichments
Add any of the following just before serving. Proportions given below are for 1 cup of soup.

- *Butter:* Remove soup from heat and stir in ½ to 1½ tablespoons butter, ½ tablespoon at a time, blending well.
- *Cream:* Whip ⅛ to ¼ cup whipping cream or crème fraîche and gently fold it into the soup. Continue heating just to warm through; do not overcook or cream will separate and curdle.
- *Egg Yolks and Cream:* Follow directions above for thickeners.

Serving Chilled Soups
Combine vegetables directly with stock and do not cook in butter. Enrich with sour cream, whipped cream or crème fraîche rather than butter. Cool soup to room temperature, then refrigerate until completely chilled. Skim off any fat before serving. If stock has gelled, beat lightly and thin as desired. Taste before serving since chilled foods often need more seasoning to heighten their flavor.

Great Hints
- For an interesting texture, stir chopped vegetables into pureed soups.
- Extend a pureed soup by adding cooked mushroom stems, pea pods, leek greens, cabbage or lettuce leaves, or asparagus, carrot or broccoli peelings before processing the mixture.
- Freeze leftover sauces and strongly flavored vegetable cooking liquid and use when preparing homemade stock.
- For variation, cook vegetables in olive oil, bacon drippings or rendered poultry fat instead of butter.

🍎 *Seafood Broths*

Fish Soup

4 servings

2 tablespoons (¼ stick) butter
1 small onion, thinly sliced
1 small carrot, cut julienne
1 small celery stalk, cut julienne
6 small mushrooms, sliced
4 cups rich fish stock
1 tablespoon fresh lemon juice
1 teaspoon fresh thyme, minced, or
 ¼ teaspoon dried thyme,
 crumbled

Salt and freshly ground pepper
¾ pound sole or other fresh white
 fish, cut lengthwise into strips ½
 inch wide
1½ tablespoons butter
1 tablespoon minced fresh parsley
Toast rounds (garnish)

Melt butter in heavy 3-quart saucepan over low heat. Add onion, carrot, celery and mushrooms and blend well. Cover and cook, stirring occasionally, until vegetables are translucent, about 10 minutes. Add fish stock and bring to simmering point. Season with lemon juice, thyme, salt and pepper. Add fish. Reduce heat until liquid is just shaking and cook until fish is opaque and is just firm to the touch, about 3 minutes. Remove from heat. Stir in remaining butter and parsley. Ladle into bowls and garnish with toast rounds.

Manhattan Clam Chowder

Make batches of this soup on weekends and freeze them to use during the week.

Makes about 6 cups

3 tablespoons butter or margarine
1 onion, finely chopped
3 6½-ounce cans chopped clams
2 8-ounce bottles clam juice
1 16-ounce can stewed tomatoes
3 ounces (½ can) tomato paste
1 medium potato, peeled and diced

3 celery stalks, diced
3 to 4 bay leaves
 Pinch of dried oregano, crumbled
 Minced fresh parsley
 Salt and freshly ground pepper
 Dash of hot pepper sauce

Melt butter or margarine in 2-quart saucepan over medium-high heat. Add onion and sautée until softened, about 10 minutes. Blend in remaining ingredients and bring to boil. Reduce heat and simmer 1 hour. Serve hot.

Clam-Tomato Broth

6 servings

2 cups clam-tomato drink
2 cups beef broth
1 cup dry white wine
½ cup dry Sherry

1 green onion, finely chopped
1 small garlic clove, halved
 Minced fresh parsley (garnish)

Combine first 4 ingredients in medium saucepan over medium-high heat and bring to boil. Reduce heat, add onion and garlic and return to boil. Let boil 1 minute. Discard garlic. Ladle soup into mugs and garnish with parsley.

🍎 Poultry and Meat Broths

Chicken and Clam Broth

2 servings

1⅔ cups rich chicken broth
⅓ cup clam juice
2 teaspoons dry Sherry
Salt and freshly ground pepper

Small spinach leaves, carrot curls and finely grated lemon peel (garnish)

Combine broth and clam juice in small saucepan and heat gently. Stir in Sherry. Taste and adjust seasoning with salt and pepper. Ladle into heated soup bowls. Garnish each serving with a spinach leaf, carrot curls and a sprinkling of grated lemon peel.

Chicken Broth

Save the chicken from this recipe for use with Cock-a-leekie Soup (page 39).

Makes 6 quarts

5 pounds chicken wings
3 pounds combined chicken necks and backs
1 3- to 3½-pound chicken, trussed

4 sprigs fresh parsley (including stems)
3 carrots, coarsely chopped
2 leeks, quartered (including 2 inches of green part)

2 celery stalks
2 bay leaves
1 onion, coarsely sliced
1 turnip, quartered
1 teaspoon salt
1 teaspoon black peppercorns, crushed
½ teaspoon dried thyme

Combine first 3 ingredients in large stockpot with enough water to cover, about 6 quarts. Bring to simmer over medium heat, skimming off foam as it rises to surface. Reduce heat and simmer uncovered for 30 minutes.

Add all remaining ingredients. Partially cover pot and simmer an additional 30 minutes or until whole chicken is cooked; remove and set whole chicken aside for another use. Continue simmering stock 2½ hours. Strain into bowl and let cool. Cover and chill overnight. When completely chilled, discard layer of fat that has formed on surface. Broth is now ready to be reheated and served, or it can be tightly covered and frozen.

Double Consommé

The egg whites and eggshells used in this recipe act as a magnet for any remaining fat.

Makes 1½ to 2 quarts

1 3- to 3½-pound chicken, trussed
2 quarts Chicken Broth (see recipe, this page)
¾ cup coarsely chopped celery
¾ cup coarsely chopped fresh parsley
¾ cup chopped leek
4 egg whites, lightly beaten

4 eggshells, crushed
Sprig of fresh tarragon

Salt
Miniature Cheese Profiteroles (garnish) (see following recipe)
Les Primeurs (garnish) (see following recipe)

Combine chicken and stock in large saucepan and simmer slowly until chicken is tender, about 45 minutes to 1 hour. Remove chicken and set aside for another use. Cool stock. Cover and chill overnight. When completely chilled, discard fat.

Combine degreased stock with all remaining ingredients except salt and garnishes in large saucepan. Bring to boil, stirring constantly with wooden spoon. Reduce heat and simmer uncovered, *without stirring*, for 30 minutes. Remove from heat and carefully ladle into tureen or bowl through strainer lined with damp paper towel. *Consommé should be absolutely clear.* Season with salt to taste. Garnish with Miniature Cheese Profiteroles or Les Primeurs.

Miniature Cheese Profiteroles

These lighter-than-air accompaniments are also excellent appetizer fare with wine and cocktails. They can be made ahead and frozen. For the consommé, allow 6 to 8 per individual bowl.

Makes about 100

½ cup water
¼ cup (½ stick) butter
   Pinch of salt
½ cup all purpose flour, sifted
2 eggs

1 tablespoon freshly grated Parmesan cheese

1 egg yolk beaten with 1 tablespoon milk

Preheat oven to 425°F. Combine butter and salt in small saucepan and bring to boil over medium heat. Remove from heat. Add flour, beating well with wooden spoon. Return to heat and continue cooking, stirring constantly, until mixture forms a mass and leaves sides of saucepan. Transfer to bowl. Beat in eggs one at a time until mixture is smooth. Blend in Parmesan.

Using pastry bag fitted with plain tip (⅛ inch), pipe small mounds of pastry the size of a pea onto baking sheet. Gently brush profiteroles with egg wash (an artist's small brush works well). Bake 5 minutes. Reduce heat to 400°F and bake until golden brown, about 5 to 6 minutes. Remove from oven and cool.

Les Primeurs (First Vegetables of the Season)

¼ cup fresh peas
2 carrots

1 turnip

Steam peas until just tender. Refresh under cold running water and set aside. Steam carrots and turnip until softened. Using miniature melon baller the size of a pea, scoop carrots and turnip to make small balls. Combine with peas and pass separately with consommé.

Soto Ayam (Chicken Soup)

6 servings

1 tablespoon peanut oil
1 piece fresh ginger (about 1 inch long), minced
2 garlic cloves, minced
1 8-ounce uncooked chicken breast half, skinned, boned and cut julienne
¼ pound cooked small shrimp
¼ teaspoon turmeric
3 cups chicken stock

¼ pound bean sprouts (fresh or rinsed and drained canned)
   Salt and freshly ground pepper

2 hard-cooked eggs, sliced
½ cup chopped green onion
2 or 3 new potatoes, boiled and sliced
   Chopped fresh parsley (garnish)

Heat oil in large saucepan over medium-high heat. Add ginger and garlic and sauté about 1 minute. Add chicken, shrimp and turmeric and stir-fry another minute. Stir in stock. Bring to boil, then reduce heat and simmer 10 minutes. Add bean sprouts and simmer 5 minutes. Season with salt and pepper.

Divide egg, green onion and potato among 6 soup bowls. Pour hot soup over and garnish with parsley.

Pizza in Brodo Alla Ninuccia (Pizza in Broth)

This light soup is the perfect beginning for an elegant dinner. Prepare the custardlike spinach pizza ahead of time so it is well chilled before serving.

6 servings

2 cups fresh spinach leaves, trimmed
1 tablespoon unsalted butter
2 cups milk
5 eggs
5 tablespoons freshly grated Parmesan cheese
4½ cups Broth (see following recipe)
Freshly grated Parmesan cheese

Preheat oven to 325°F. Generously butter 8 × 12-inch baking dish. Wash spinach thoroughly and cook until wilted, using only water clinging to the leaves. Drain well and squeeze out as much water as possible. Melt butter in small skillet over medium heat, add spinach and sauté for 3 to 5 minutes.

Bring kettle filled with water to boil.

Transfer spinach to processor or blender. Add milk, eggs and Parmesan and mix until pureed. Turn into prepared dish. Place in larger pan and set in oven. Add boiling water to fill pan almost to the top and bake uncovered for 45 minutes.

Carefully remove pans from oven and discard water bath. Cool pizza completely at room temperature, then cover and refrigerate until serving time.

To serve, cut pizza lengthwise into ½-inch strips, using pizza cutter or very sharp knife, then cut crosswise into ½-inch squares. Divide evenly among 6 soup bowls. Bring broth to boil in saucepan. Ladle evenly over chilled pizza squares and serve immediately with Parmesan cheese on the side.

Broth

Makes about 3 quarts

1 3-pound stewing chicken
1 large onion
4 whole cloves
3½ quarts water
1 pound chicken giblets or mixture of giblets and hearts
2 veal bones
2 beef bones with marrow
4 celery stalks
1 large carrot
2 sprigs parsley
1 bunch fresh dill, green leaves only
1 medium tomato
12 whole black peppercorns
2 lemon slices
½ cup Sherry

Place chicken in large pot. Stud onion with cloves. Add to pot with all remaining ingredients except Sherry. Bring to boil, reduce heat and simmer uncovered about 2 hours. Stir in Sherry.

Line colander with layers of cheesecloth. Set over large bowl. Ladle stock into colander to strain into bowl.

Cooked vegetables from stock can be pureed and served as soup. Add a spoonful of yogurt, tomato puree or chopped spinach or a dash of Worcestershire sauce, if desired.

Nona's Salad Egg-Drop Soup

*Serve with a Bardolino or
Zinfandel.*

6 to 8 servings

3 to 4 tablespoons butter or olive
   oil
3 large onions, finely chopped
2 small zucchini, finely chopped
2 carrots, finely chopped
1 celery stalk, finely chopped
1 small garlic clove, minced
1 bay leaf
1 tablespoon fresh basil or 1
   teaspoon dried, crumbled
¾ teaspoon fresh oregano or ¼
   teaspoon dried, crumbled

¼ teaspoon fresh rosemary or
   generous pinch of dried,
   crumbled
8 to 10 cups chicken stock
   (preferably homemade)
6 large romaine or escarole leaves,
   shredded
6 eggs
   Salt and freshly ground pepper
1 cup grated Parmesan cheese

Heat butter or oil in 5- to 6-quart saucepan over medium-low heat. Add onion,
zucchini, carrot, celery, garlic, bay leaf, basil, oregano and rosemary. Cover and
cook, stirring occasionally, until vegetables are wilted, about 10 minutes. Stir in
chicken stock and romaine or escarole leaves. Increase heat to medium-high and
boil until vegetables are tender, about 10 minutes.

    Whisk eggs lightly in medium bowl. Remove stock from heat. Gradually
whisk in eggs, stirring slowly to form thin, firm threads. Season with salt and
pepper to taste. Transfer soup to tureen or individual bowls. Serve immediately.
Pass cheese separately.

Paul Bocuse Soupe Aux Truffes Elysée (Truffle Soup Elysée)

1 serving

2 tablespoons Brunoise (see
   following recipe)
½ ounce cooked chicken breast,
   diced (about 3 tablespoons)
1¾ ounces fresh or canned truffle,
   sliced*
1 tablespoon truffle juice
1 tablespoon brown sauce
1 tablespoon dry vermouth
⅓ cup rich beef consommé
   (homemade or commercial),
   slightly chilled

   Freshly ground pepper
½ ounce foie gras, diced (about 1½
   tablespoons)**

1 7 × 7-inch square puff pastry
   (pâte feuilletée)

1 egg

Place first 9 ingredients *in order given* in deep 2-cup soup bowl 4 inches in diameter; *do not stir* (the soup should be about 1 inch from rim of bowl). Refrigerate
until well chilled.

    Roll pastry ⅛ inch thick. Cut out 6-inch circle and gently lay over top of
bowl, leaving 1-inch overhang. Seal by pressing firmly to *sides* of bowl (do not
crimp to rim; pastry must be allowed to rise freely). Carefully transfer bowl to
baking sheet. Refrigerate until pastry is firm. Cover completely with plastic wrap
and chill overnight.

    About 30 minutes before serving, position rack in lower third of oven and
preheat to 400°F. Lightly beat egg and use to brush pastry for glaze. Bake until
pastry is puffed and golden, about 15 to 20 minutes. Serve immediately.

Brunoise

Makes about ¾ cup

1½ tablespoons butter	1 celery stalk (without leaves), finely diced
6 mushrooms, finely diced	
1 carrot, finely diced	1 small onion, finely diced

Melt butter in small saucepan over low heat. Add vegetables, cover and simmer until vegetables are heightened in color but still crisp; do not overcook.

*Small dried shiitake (Japanese mushrooms) can be substituted for truffle. Soak 1¾ ounces (about 15 small) mushrooms until softened in enough water barely to cover, turning frequently to aid rehydration. Drain, reserving liquid to use in place of truffle juice. Press mushrooms with paper towel in order to remove excess moisture.

**Domestic liver pâté can be substituted for imported foie gras.

Consommé

This stock should be prepared ahead and chilled to facilitate removal of fat.

Makes 3 to 4 quarts.

Meats
- 2 pounds beef soup bones
- 2 pounds chicken bones, giblets and backs
- 3 pounds beef (stew meat, short ribs or chuck)
- 1 3-pound fryer chicken, cut in half lengthwise

Vegetables
- 3 stalks celery with leaves
- 3 carrots, unpeeled, scrubbed
- 3 leeks, cleaned and split (reserve green tops)
- 1 large onion, unpeeled, root end removed
- 2 parsnips or turnips
- 6 parsley sprigs
- 5 garlic cloves, unpeeled, lightly crushed

Seasonings
- 3 sprigs fresh dill or 2 teaspoons dried
- 1 teaspoon thyme
- 2 bay leaves
- 6 whole cloves
- 1 teaspoon whole allspice
- 3 ⅛-inch slices fresh ginger or 1 teaspoon ground
- 1 teaspoon peppercorns
- 2 teaspoons salt

Arrange beef and chicken bones in bottom of 12- to 16-quart stockpot. Add beef, celery, carrots, leeks (white part only), onion, parsnips or turnips, parsley, garlic and seasonings. Add enough cold water to cover ¾ of contents. Slowly bring to a simmer and cook uncovered for 1 hour.

Add chicken halves and cover soup with green leek tops to keep flavors from evaporating. Simmer 1 hour longer or until soup has a rich flavor.

Let vegetables and meat cool in broth. When cool, remove meat and bones. Reserve meat. With a wooden spoon, press vegetables through strainer, returning juices to soup. Strain broth into 6-quart bowl or pan. Return meat to broth. Refrigerate overnight.

Discard solid layer of fat on top of chilled soup. Reheat stock and adjust seasonings to taste.

Variation 1
Pot-au-Feu: The traditional French family-style boiled dinner. Reheat chicken and beef in stock. Add your favorite fresh vegetables and simmer until tender.

Variation 2
All-Chicken Stock: Substitute 2 pounds chicken bones and another 3 pounds chicken for beef bones and beef.

Home-Style Broth

Try keeping two plastic bags in the freezer—one for the vegetable scraps and one for meats and poultry. When the bags are full, it's time to make broth. Fresh herbs, onions and wine give added flavor.

Makes 6 quarts

3 to 4 pounds cooked or uncooked meat bones and/or poultry bones and meat scraps
3 to 4 cups vegetable peelings (such as stems, tops and bottoms of celery, carrot, parsnip, rutabaga, turnip, parsley and spinach)
3 large onions, unpeeled, coarsely chopped
1 cup dry white wine
1 bay leaf
¾ teaspoon fresh thyme or ¼ teaspoon dried, crumbled
Water

Combine bones, peelings, onion, wine, bay leaf and thyme in 10- to 12-quart stockpot. Add enough water to cover ingredients by 2 inches. Bring to slow simmer over medium-high heat, skimming foam as it rises to surface. Reduce heat, cover partially and let simmer 8 to 10 hours, adding more water as necessary. Strain into large bowl. Refrigerate overnight. Discard fat from surface. Pour broth into small containers. Cover and refrigerate up to 4 days or freeze up to 4 months. Reheat to serve.

For easy long-term storage, freeze broth in ice cube trays, then transfer cubes to plastic bags when solidly frozen.

Brown Beef Broth

Makes about 6 quarts

5 pounds beef bones (combination of marrow bones, short ribs and beef shanks)
3 pounds veal bones
2 pounds veal shanks
2 pounds chicken wings

2 onions, thinly sliced
2 carrots, thinly sliced

5 sprigs fresh parsley (including stems)
2 to 3 sprigs fresh thyme or 1 teaspoon dried
2 leeks, coarsely chopped
1 celery stalk (including leaves), cut into chunks
1 teaspoon black peppercorns, crushed
1 teaspoon salt

Preheat oven to between 400°F and 425°F. Arrange first 4 ingredients in large shallow roasting pan. Roast until browned, turning occasionally to promote even cooking, about 1 hour.

Transfer bones to large stockpot and add enough water to cover, about 6 quarts. Bring to simmer. During first 30 minutes of cooking time, skim off any foam that accumulates on surface.

Meanwhile, pour off all but 2 tablespoons fat from roasting pan. Add onion and carrot. Place pan over direct heat and brown vegetables slowly, stirring constantly with wooden spoon. When vegetables are golden, add about 1½ cups water to pan and deglaze, using wooden spatula to scrape up all browned bits clinging to pan.

Transfer pan contents to stockpot. Add remaining ingredients and blend well. Simmer slowly, either uncovered or partially covered, for 8 hours. Strain into large container and cool. Cover and chill overnight. When completely chilled, discard layer of fat that has formed on surface. Stock is now ready for immediate use, or it can be frozen.

❦ *Vegetable Cream Soups*

Cream of Artichoke Soup

4 servings

½ cup plus 2 tablespoons (1¼ sticks) unsalted butter
½ cup chopped carrot
½ cup chopped celery
½ cup chopped onion
½ cup chopped mushrooms

¼ cup unbleached all purpose flour
1 cup chicken broth
2 8½-ounce cans (drained weight) quartered artichoke hearts, juice reserved
1 bay leaf

¾ teaspoon salt
½ teaspoon freshly ground pepper
¼ teaspoon ground red pepper
¼ teaspoon dried thyme, crumbled, or ¾ teaspoon minced fresh
¼ teaspoon dried oregano, crumbled, or ¾ teaspoon minced fresh
¼ teaspoon sage
Pinch of Hungarian sweet paprika

1 cup whipping cream

Melt 2 tablespoons butter in large heavy skillet over medium heat. Add carrot, celery, onion and mushrooms and sauté until vegetables are soft and onion is translucent, about 15 minutes. Set aside.

Melt remaining butter in large stockpot over low heat. Add flour and cook, stirring constantly, for 5 minutes. Stir in vegetables. Add broth in slow, steady stream, stirring constantly. Add artichoke hearts with juice, bay leaf, salt, pepper, ground red pepper, thyme, oregano, sage and paprika and stir through. Increase heat to medium and simmer 30 minutes, stirring occasionally.

Beat cream in small bowl just until frothy. Blend into soup. Heat through; *do not boil.* Adjust seasoning. Serve immediately.

Herbed Carrot Cream with Peas

Serve with a delicate California Johannisberg Riesling.

6 to 8 servings

¼ cup (½ stick) butter
1 pound carrots, shredded
1 large bunch green onions (about 8), minced
6 large shallots, minced
1 small potato, peeled and finely chopped
1 small garlic clove, minced
1½ teaspoons fresh tarragon or ¼ to ½ teaspoon dried, crumbled
1½ teaspoons fresh chervil or ¼ to ½

teaspoon dried, crumbled
¾ teaspoon fresh marjoram or ¼ teaspoon dried, crumbled
¼ teaspoon fresh thyme or generous pinch of dried, crumbled
2 quarts rich chicken stock

1 cup whipping cream
1 10-ounce package frozen tiny peas, thawed
Salt and freshly ground pepper

Melt butter in heavy 5- to 6-quart saucepan over medium-low heat. Add carrot, green onion, shallot, potato, garlic, tarragon, chervil, marjoram and thyme. Cover and cook, stirring occasionally, until vegetables are wilted, about 10 to 15 minutes. Pour in chicken stock, increase heat to medium-high and bring to boil. Boil uncovered until potato is tender, about 15 minutes. *(Can be prepared 1 day ahead, covered and refrigerated.)*

Transfer soup to processor or blender in batches and puree. Return to stockpot and reheat to simmer. Add cream and peas and cook just until heated through. Season with salt and pepper to taste. Serve immediately.

Curried Spring Asparagus Soup

A simple yet marvelous way to mark the change of the seasons in your menu. Vary this recipe by adding a touch of finely minced fresh herbs, such as dill or tarragon. Serve with buttered French bread.

6 to 8 servings

1 pound fresh asparagus
6 cups chicken stock or bouillon (preferably homemade)

¼ cup (½ stick) butter
3 tablespoons flour

3 large egg yolks

1 teaspoon curry powder or more to taste
1 cup whipping cream
Salt and freshly ground white pepper

Remove and discard woody ends from asparagus stalks. Scrape spears with vegetable peeler. Cut off tips and reserve. Dice stalks and combine with stock in 4-quart saucepan. Bring to boil and cook uncovered for 10 minutes or until very tender. Cool, then puree in blender or food processor. Set aside.

Melt butter over low heat in large heavy saucepan. Add flour and cook, stirring constantly, 2 to 3 minutes. Stir in puree and bring to boil over medium heat. Add asparagus tips. Cover and simmer 10 minutes or until tips are tender.

While soup is simmering, thoroughly combine yolks, curry and cream with whisk. Add to soup and heat through but do not let boil. Season to taste with salt and pepper. Serve hot.

Cream of Carrot and Rice Soup

6 to 8 servings

3 tablespoons butter
½ pound carrots (about 2 large), washed and thinly sliced
1 medium onion, thinly sliced
1 quart (4 cups) chicken stock
¼ cup long-grain white rice
1 teaspoon salt

½ teaspoon freshly ground white pepper

1 cup whipping cream
1 tablespoon minced fresh parsley or chives (garnish)

Melt butter in heavy 3-quart saucepan over low heat. Add carrot and onion, cover and cook about 15 minutes, stirring occasionally to prevent sticking. Stir in stock, rice, salt and pepper. Cover and simmer until vegetables are tender, about 30 to 40 minutes.

Transfer to processor or blender in batches and puree. Return to saucepan. Stir in cream (if soup is too thick, thin with stock or water). Place over low heat and bring to simmer. Taste and adjust seasoning. Ladle soup into tureen and garnish as desired.

Celery and Almond Soup

2 servings

2 tablespoons (¼ stick) butter
½ pound celery (about 3 large stalks), chopped
¼ teaspoon curry powder or to taste
1 cup chicken broth
2 teaspoons minced fresh parsley

1 cup milk
Salt and freshly ground pepper

2 tablespoons whipping cream
2 tablespoons slivered almonds, toasted

Melt butter in medium saucepan over low heat. Add celery and curry and cook about 10 minutes, stirring occasionally. Stir in broth and parsley and bring to boil over high heat. Reduce heat to low, cover and simmer 20 minutes. Blend in milk, salt and pepper.

Transfer to blender and mix until almost smooth (there will be tiny crunchy bits of celery that give the soup a pleasing texture). Return to low heat and warm through. Stir in cream and almonds just before serving.

Celery and Watercress Soup

Serve hot or chilled.

4 servings

3 tablespoons vegetable oil (preferably cold-pressed safflower)
1 bunch celery (including leaves), sliced
1 medium-size yellow onion, sliced
1 teaspoon finely chopped garlic
Freshly ground white pepper
2 tablespoons flour (preferably whole wheat pastry flour)
1½ cups chicken or vegetable stock or 1½ cups water mixed with 1½ teaspoons tamari soy sauce
½ bunch watercress (including stems), coarsely chopped

1 cup double-strength reconstituted nonfat dry milk or whipping cream
1 tablespoon finely chopped fresh dill or 1½ teaspoons dried dillweed or 2 teaspoons finely chopped fresh tarragon or 1 teaspoon dried, crumbled
Herb or vegetable salt
Leaves from 3 or 4 large sprigs fresh watercress (garnish)

Heat oil in heavy 3-quart saucepan over medium heat. Add celery, onion and garlic and cook until celery is tender, about 10 to 15 minutes. Season with pepper. Remove from heat and stir in flour. Place over medium heat, add stock and bring to boil, stirring constantly. Blend in watercress. Transfer mixture to processor or blender in batches and puree until smooth (or press through fine strainer).

Return puree to saucepan. Stir in milk and dill or tarragon. Add herb salt to taste. Place over low and heat through (or let cool, cover and refrigerate). Garnish each serving with watercress.

Southern-Style Corn Chowder

12 servings

2 ounces lean salt pork, diced
8 tablespoons (1 stick) unsalted butter
3 large onions, chopped
1 large green pepper, seeded and diced
8 medium potatoes, peeled and diced
4 cups milk

2 cups whipping cream
5 cups fresh corn kernels or 5 cups thawed frozen kernels, cooked until tender
¼ cup minced fresh parsley
Salt and freshly ground pepper
Freshly grated nutmeg
Crisp-cooked bacon, crumbled (garnish)

Cook salt pork in large skillet over low heat until 2 tablespoons fat have been rendered. Remove any remaining solid pork. Add 2 tablespoons butter to skillet and let melt. Increase heat to medium, add onion and sauté until pale golden. Add green pepper and sauté briefly until just tender but still bright green. Remove from heat.

Cook diced potatoes in enough boiling salted water to cover until they are tender but still hold their shape. Drain well.

Combine milk and cream in large saucepan and heat slowly. When hot, add remaining ingredients except butter and bacon. Bring just to simmer, then remove from heat and let stand at least 3 hours to cool and thicken. *(Soup may be prepared to this point, covered and stored overnight in refrigerator.)*

Just before serving, reheat soup gently. Carefully stir in remaining butter, being careful not to break or mash vegetables. Thin with milk if desired. Pass bacon separately to garnish each serving.

Cream of Corn Soup with Shellfish Butter

This soup is best made with young unripe, or "green," corn. The Shellfish Butter should be made from crayfish, but shrimp, crab or lobster can be substituted. The butter should be added just before serving soup so that it softens but doesn't separate.

6 to 8 servings

6 cups rich chicken stock
12 ears very young fresh corn (do not use canned or frozen), kernels cut from cob
6 egg yolks

½ cup whipping cream
Salt and freshly ground pepper
Shellfish Butter (see following recipe)

Bring stock to boiling point in heavy saucepan. Add corn and let boil 1 minute. Remove from heat and let stand 5 minutes. Puree corn with some of the liquid in processor or blender. Mix puree back into stock, then strain through fine sieve, mashing to extract as much liquid as possible. Combine yolks and cream and mix well. Slowly blend in 1 cup hot liquid, then pour back into pan, stirring constantly. Season with salt and pepper to taste. Reheat carefully, stirring constantly, until slightly thickened; *do not let soup boil.* Serve immediately with Shellfish Butter and a few slices of the shellfish.

Shellfish Butter

1 cup mirepoix (equal parts finely chopped carrot, celery and onion)
½ teaspoon finely minced thyme
½ teaspoon finely minced fresh parsley

1 pound shellfish (crayfish, shrimp, crab or lobster)
½ cup fish stock or white wine
Salt and freshly ground pepper
1 cup (2 sticks) unsalted butter

Combine mirepoix and herbs in heavy saucepan. Cover and let sweat over very low heat about 10 minutes. Add shellfish, stock or wine, and salt and pepper to taste. Cover and cook over medium heat until shellfish are done, about 5 minutes. Remove shells. Place shells in processor, or use mortar and pestle, and puree, or pound, until smooth. Add butter and blend completely (the butter should take on the flavor and color of the shells). Force through fine sieve (consistency will be like that of whipped butter). Shape into small balls with teaspoon and refrigerate until shortly before ready to drop into hot soup (butter should be soft enough so it slowly melts into soup as it is eaten). Slice some of the shellfish and set aside to garnish soup; use remainder as desired.

Cauliflower Soup

Makes 4 cups

2 tablespoons (¼ stick) butter
½ cup minced onion or 1 small leek (white part only), minced, or ¼ cup minced shallot or ½ cup minced green onion (white part only)
1 medium cauliflower, cut into ½-inch pieces (about 4 cups florets)
1½ cups (about) chicken stock, milk or water

1 cup whipping cream or to taste
Salt and freshly ground pepper
Freshly grated nutmeg
1 to 2 tablespoons Port, Sherry, Madeira or dry red or white wine (optional)
Enrichment (optional) (see box, pages 6–7)

Melt butter in heavy 2-quart saucepan over low heat. Add onion or leek, cover and cook 10 minutes (5 minutes for shallot or green onion), stirring occasionally. Add cauliflower, cover and cook 5 minutes, stirring halfway through cooking time. Pour in enough stock, milk or water barely to cover ingredients. Cover pan partially and bring to boil. Let boil until cauliflower is tender, about 10 minutes. Transfer to blender or processor in batches and puree, or pass mixture through fine disk of food mill. (If desired, press puree through fine strainer for even smoother texture.) Thin soup with cream and season with salt, pepper and nutmeg. Stir in Port or other wine and enrich as desired. Ladle into bowls and serve.

Soup can be kept warm in top of double boiler or in bain-marie, but do not add enrichment until just before serving.

Cream of Chestnut Soup

6 to 8 servings

3 tablespoons rendered chicken fat or duck fat
2 large Bermuda onions, thinly sliced
2 large carrots, finely diced
1 3-inch cinnamon stick

2 pounds fresh chestnuts, peeled

6 cups rich chicken stock
Pinch of mace
Pinch of freshly grated nutmeg
Salt and freshly ground white pepper
1 cup whipping cream

Melt fat in heavy 3-quart saucepan over medium heat. Add onion, carrot and cinnamon stick. Cover partially and cook until vegetables are caramelized, about 45 to 60 minutes, stirring frequently toward end of cooking time to prevent them from scorching.

Discard cinnamon stick. Blend in chestnuts and stock. Cook until chestnuts are tender, about 15 to 20 minutes. Transfer soup to processor or blender in batches and puree. Return puree to saucepan and stir in mace, nutmeg, salt and pepper. Whisk in cream. Place over very low heat and heat through but do not allow to boil. Taste and adjust seasoning. Serve hot.

Mushroom Soup

A very special rendition, richly flavored with dux-elles and lemon.

4 to 6 servings

1 pound mushrooms
Juice of ½ lemon
1 tablespoon butter
2 tablespoons minced shallot
½ bay leaf
¼ teaspoon dried thyme

2 cups whipping cream

1½ cups chicken stock
1 teaspoon salt
½ teaspoon freshly ground pepper
1 teaspoon cornstarch dissolved in 1 tablespoon water
1 tablespoon chopped fresh parsley (garnish)

Chop mushrooms with lemon juice in processor. Melt butter in large skillet over medium heat. Add shallot and sauté lightly. Add mushrooms, bay leaf and thyme and cook, stirring frequently, until liquid is evaporated, about 10 minutes.

Blend in cream, chicken stock, salt and pepper and bring to boil. Reduce heat and simmer 20 minutes. Add dissolved cornstarch and simmer 10 minutes longer. Adjust seasoning. Ladle into heated bowls and sprinkle with parsley.

Mushroom Bisque

8 servings

¼ cup (½ stick) butter
1 small onion, chopped
1 celery stalk, chopped
¾ pound mushrooms, sliced
1 small potato, peeled and diced
1 cup water
1¼ teaspoons salt
¾ teaspoon minced fresh thyme or

¼ teaspoon dried, crumbled
Pinch of freshly ground white pepper
2 cups milk
¾ cup whipping cream
¼ cup dry Sherry
2 teaspoons tamari soy sauce
Sour cream (garnish)

Melt butter in large heavy saucepan over medium-low heat. Add onion and celery. Cover and cook until transparent, about 10 minutes. Stir in mushrooms and cook until softened, about 6 minutes. Add potato, water, salt, thyme and pepper. Increase heat and simmer until potato is very soft, about 15 minutes. Puree mixture in processor or blender until smooth, stopping to scrape down sides of container. Return mixture to saucepan. Add milk, cream, Sherry and soy sauce. Heat through; *do not boil*. Ladle into bowls. Garnish with sour cream.

Pimiento Soup with Vermouth

2 servings

1 tablespoon butter
¼ cup chopped onion
1 tablespoon flour
1½ cups chicken broth

1 2-ounce jar pimientos, drained
½ cup whipping cream
2 tablespoons dry white vermouth
Freshly ground white pepper

Melt butter in medium saucepan over medium-high heat. Add onion and sauté until soft. Stir in flour, reduce heat to low and cook for 2 minutes. Add broth and pimientos and continue cooking until soup has thickened. Transfer to processor or blender and mix until smooth. Return soup to saucepan. Stir in cream, vermouth and pepper and heat through.

Trianon Dill Pickle Soup

6 to 8 servings

3 tablespoons butter
3 ounces onion, cut julienne
½ cup white wine
⅓ cup plus 1 tablespoon all purpose flour
5 cups water
1½ cups marinade from pickles

4 large dill pickles, cut julienne
2 teaspoons dried dillweed
Whipping cream (optional)
Poultry seasoning
Salt and freshly ground white pepper
Diced pickles (garnish)

Melt butter in large pot or Dutch oven over medium heat. Add onion and sauté until soft. Add wine and continue cooking until almost all liquid evaporates. Reduce heat and stir in flour; do not brown. Combine water and pickle marinade and whisk into mixture all at once. Increase heat and bring to boil, stirring constantly, until soup thickens. Add pickles and dill. Stir in cream if lighter color is desired. Season with poultry seasoning, salt and pepper to taste. Garnish each serving with diced pickles.

Pine Nut Soup

6 to 8 servings

3 tablespoons butter
¼ cup plus 1 tablespoon shelled
   pine nuts
1 small onion, chopped
3 tablespoons all purpose flour

⅛ teaspoon nutmeg
2 10¾-ounce cans chicken broth
1 10-ounce package frozen chopped
   spinach, thawed
2 cups milk

Melt butter in medium skillet over medium-high heat. Add pine nuts and sauté until golden. Transfer to paper towels using slotted spoon and drain well. Chop nuts in processor or blender. Add onion to butter remaining in skillet and cook over medium-high heat until tender, about 10 minutes. Add flour and nutmeg and stir over low heat 3 minutes. Blend in 3 tablespoons nuts. Add broth and bring to boil. Add spinach and milk. Reduce heat and simmer 5 minutes. Add remaining nuts. Ladle into bowls and serve hot.

Potato-Leek Soup

6 to 8 servings

8 cups chicken broth
  Salt
6 medium potatoes, peeled and
   diced
6 celery stalks, cut into 1-inch
   pieces
3 medium leeks (including ⅔ of
   green part), trimmed, well
   washed and cut into 1-inch pieces

2 tablespoons (¼ stick) butter or
   margarine
1 cup sour cream
  Chopped fresh chives (optional
   garnish)

Combine broth with salt to taste in 3- to 4-quart saucepan over medium-high heat. Add potato, celery and leek. Reduce heat to medium, cover and cook until vegetables are tender, about 20 minutes. Puree vegetables in batches with some liquid in processor or blender. Return puree to saucepan, blending well. Place over medium heat. Add butter, stirring until melted. Ladle into bowls. Top each with some sour cream and chives. Serve immediately.

Curried Pumpkin Soup

6 to 8 servings

2 tablespoons (¼ stick) butter
¼ cup finely chopped onion
1 tablespoon all purpose flour
1½ teaspoons curry powder
2 10¾-ounce cans chicken broth
1 16-ounce can pumpkin
1 teaspoon brown sugar

¼ teaspoon salt
  Freshly ground pepper
  Freshly grated nutmeg
1 cup milk
  Minced chives or parsley
  Lowfat plain yogurt (garnish)

Melt butter in 3-quart saucepan over medium-high heat. Add onion and sauté until translucent, about 5 minutes. Mix in flour and curry powder and cook until bubbly, about 2 minutes. Remove from heat and gradually stir in broth. Add pumpkin, brown sugar, salt, pepper and nutmeg. Cook over medium heat, stirring constantly until thickened. Blend in milk and continue cooking until warmed through; do not boil. Ladle into bowls. Sprinkle with chives or parsley. Garnish with yogurt. Serve immediately.

Green and Yellow Squash Soup

Any type of squash can be used, but a mixture of yellow and green is best for a more delicate combination. You can also use zucchini only, but choose oversized, meatier ones, discarding seeds. Finish the zucchini version with a dash of Worcestershire sauce or a dollop of yogurt in place of the cream.

6 to 8 servings

Soup
2 to 3 cups peeled, cubed pumpkin
2 to 3 cups peeled, cubed zucchini
2 potatoes, peeled and cubed
1 large onion, sliced
1½ to 2 cups salt-free chicken broth or bouillon
5 tablespoons olive oil
3 sprigs fresh parsley

1 to 2 garlic cloves

Pesticino
2 fresh basil leaves
2 fresh mint leaves
1 garlic clove
¼ cup whipping cream
1 tablespoon minced fresh parsley

Combine all ingredients for soup in large saucepan. Cover and cook over low heat, stirring occasionally, until vegetables are soft, about 45 minutes to 1 hour, adding more broth if necessary.

Meanwhile, mince basil, mint and garlic and transfer to small bowl. Stir in cream and parsley and mix well.

Transfer soup to processor or blender in batches and puree. Return puree to saucepan. Stir in pesticino. Reheat gently just until warmed through, but *do not boil*. Serve immediately.

Quantity of vegetables can be increased. Add 1 tablespoon oil for every additional cup of pumpkin or zucchini.

Soup base can be frozen. Thaw before adding pesticino. Reheat gently.

Russian Sorrel Soup

6 to 8 servings

6 to 8 cups chicken broth or bouillon
3 medium potatoes, peeled and diced
1½ pounds fresh sorrel, well washed, stems removed (about 8 cups packed)

Salt and freshly ground white pepper

1 cup Crème Fraîche (see following recipe) or sour cream (garnish)
2 tablespoons finely minced chives (garnish)

Bring chicken broth to a boil in 4-quart pot. Add potato and cook over medium heat 15 to 20 minutes or until tender. Add sorrel to stock and continue simmering another 10 minutes.

Puree soup in blender or processor until completely smooth. Press through fine sieve. Return to pot and reheat. Season to taste with salt and pepper.

Combine crème fraîche or sour cream with chives in bowl and set aside.

Pour soup into individual bowls and top each with a spoonful of cream and chive mixture. Serve hot.

For an interesting variation, add 1 cup of packed julienned sorrel leaves to the hot soup. Let leaves "melt" in soup 1 or 2 minutes, but don't let soup return to a boil. Serve from a soup tureen with cream and chives on the side.

Crème Fraîche

Crème fraîche will keep well one to two weeks.

2 cups fresh whipping cream

2 tablespoons buttermilk

Combine whipping cream and buttermilk in a jar and whisk mixture until well blended. Cover and let stand in warm place to thicken for 24 hours. Refrigerate until ready to use.

Peasant Soup

Serve hot or chilled.

8 servings

6 cups water
4 large potatoes, peeled and sliced (if skins are new and thin, scrub potatoes but do not peel)
3 large yellow onions, sliced
3 large celery stalks, sliced
1 teaspoon sea salt or 2 teaspoons coarse salt
1 teaspoon herb or vegetable salt
¼ cup olive oil (preferably cold-pressed)
¼ cup vegetable oil (preferably cold-pressed safflower)

1 pound fresh spinach or sorrel (including stems), well washed (or mixture of any leftover greens, such as spinach, lettuce, parsley, celery leaf or watercress)
1 cup double-strength reconstituted nonfat dry milk or half and half or sour cream
1 cup garlic or cheese whole wheat croutons, fried (garnish)

Combine water, potato, onion, celery, salts and oils in heavy 4-quart saucepan. Cover and cook over medium heat until potato is tender, about 10 to 15 minutes. Remove from heat and stir in spinach or sorrel, blending thoroughly.

Transfer mixture to processor or blender in batches and puree (or press through fine strainer). Return puree to saucepan and stir in milk. Adjust seasoning. Ladle into bowls and pass garlic or cheese croutons separately.

Cheesy Cream of Spinach Soup

6 servings

3 tablespoons butter
1 tablespoon oil
1 small onion, minced
2 10-ounce packages frozen chopped spinach, thawed
2 tablespoons all purpose flour
1 14½-ounce can chicken broth

2 cups half and half
½ teaspoon freshly ground white pepper
Freshly grated nutmeg
½ pound bacon, chopped and crisply cooked
1 cup grated cheddar cheese

Melt butter with oil in large saucepan over medium heat. Add onion and cook until transparent, about 5 minutes. Press spinach in large strainer, reserving liquid. Add spinach to onion and mix well. Sprinkle with flour and cook, stirring frequently, 3 minutes. Blend in broth and reserved spinach liquid and bring to simmer. Cook 10 minutes. Stir in half and half, pepper and nutmeg and simmer gently 5 minutes. Add bacon and cheese. Ladle soup into bowls and serve hot.

Zucchini Soup

2 servings

1 tablespoon butter
2 zucchini, grated (about 2 cups)
2 tablespoons chopped onion
2 tablespoons minced fresh parsley
1½ cups milk

¼ cup whipping cream
Salt and freshly ground white pepper
Minced fresh parsley (garnish)

Melt butter in medium saucepan over low heat. Stir in zucchini, onion and 2 tablespoons parsley. Cover and cook, stirring frequently, until zucchini is tender, about 7 to 10 minutes. Remove from heat and blend in milk. Place over medium heat and cook, stirring constantly, until milk is almost boiling. Reduce heat and simmer, stirring occasionally, about 20 minutes. Transfer soup to blender and puree until smooth. Return to saucepan. Add cream and stir over medium heat until heated through. Season with salt and pepper. Garnish with parsley.

Le Pavillon's Gin Tomato Soup

4 servings

1 package unflavored gelatin
¼ cup cold water

1½ pounds tomatoes, peeled and seeded
3 garlic cloves
Salt and freshly ground pepper
Sugar
Paprika

3 slices bacon, cut into thin strips
¼ cup plus 2 tablespoons (¾ stick) butter, room temperature
Pinch of thyme

2 ounces mushrooms, sliced
¼ cup (2 ounces) gin
¼ cup plus 2 tablespoons whipping cream

Sprinkle gelatin over water in small saucepan and let stand until softened. Stir over low heat until gelatin is dissolved. Remove from heat and set aside.

Puree tomato and 2 garlic cloves in blender until smooth. Taste and season with salt, pepper, sugar and paprika. Add softened gelatin and blend well. Spoon into small cups or molds and chill until aspic is set.

Sauté bacon in small skillet over medium heat until crisp. Drain well. Whip butter with whisk in small bowl. Blend in bacon. Mince remaining garlic clove and add to butter with thyme.

Melt butter-bacon mixture in large skillet over medium-high heat. Add mushrooms and sauté until golden. Warm gin in small saucepan, then add to skillet and flambé. Reduce heat, add aspic and bring to simmer, stirring constantly, so aspic will melt and blend into soup. Stir in cream. Cook until heated through. Serve immediately.

Italian Tomato and Red Pepper Soup

12 servings

2 tablespoons (¼ stick) unsalted butter
1 tablespoon olive oil
3 large onions, thinly sliced
6 large sweet red peppers, seeded and thinly sliced
6 large garlic cloves
1 large carrot, diced
½ teaspoon dried thyme
½ teaspoon dried oregano
Bouquet garni (bay leaf, celery leaves, leek greens, parsley sprigs, 2-inch strip of orange peel

Salt
Cayenne pepper

12 large ripe tomatoes, peeled, seeded and chopped, or 6 cups canned tomatoes, drained, peeled and chopped
3 tablespoons dry Sherry
1 tablespoon red wine vinegar
5 cups defatted chicken stock
Freshly ground pepper

Puree Saint-Germain (see following recipe)

Melt butter with oil in large nonaluminum saucepan over medium heat. Add onion and cook until it just begins to turn golden; *do not brown*. Add next 8 ingredients and blend. Reduce heat to low, cover and cook 10 minutes, stirring a few times.

Add tomato, Sherry and vinegar and cook uncovered, stirring frequently, for 10 minutes. Stir in stock. Bring to boil, reduce heat and simmer 10 minutes. Season to taste with pepper.

Discard bouquet garni, pressing out any liquid into soup. Set large sieve over bowl and strain soup, pressing vegetables through sieve with back of spoon.

Return to saucepan and heat. To serve, swirl several spoonfuls of Puree Saint-Germain through each portion, or serve soup and puree separately and let guests help themselves at the buffet table.

Puree Saint-Germain

Makes about 3½ to 4 cups

4 cups fresh or thawed frozen green peas
4 green onions, thinly sliced

½ to 1 cup whipping cream
Salt and freshly ground pepper

In medium saucepan, cook peas and onion in boiling salted water just until tender. Drain, refresh under cold water and drain again. Transfer to processor or blender, add ½ cup cream and puree. Thin with additional cream until same consistency as soup. Season with salt and pepper. Serve hot.

Curried Cream of Vegetable Soup

4 to 6 servings

3 carrots, chopped
½ head cauliflower, chopped
1 medium onion, chopped
1 medium potato, peeled and chopped
1 tablespoon chopped fresh parsley

2 chicken bouillon cubes
1 cup whipping cream
½ teaspoon curry powder
¼ teaspoon Worcestershire sauce
Freshly ground white pepper

Bring 3 cups water to boil in 2-quart saucepan over medium-high heat. Add carrot, cauliflower, onion, potato, parsley and bouillon cubes and return to boil. Continue cooking until vegetables are tender, about 15 minutes. Transfer mixture to blender or processor in batches and puree until smooth. Return to saucepan. Blend in whipping cream. Mix in remaining ingredients. Place over medium heat and cook until heated through. Ladle into bowls. Serve hot.

❦ *Seafood Cream Soups*

Crab Bisque

6 servings

¾ cup (1½ sticks) butter
1½ medium onions, minced
1 medium carrot, finely minced
½ stick celery, finely minced
1 teaspoon flour
1 teaspoon chopped fresh parsley
1 teaspoon seafood seasoning

¼ teaspoon celery salt
⅛ teaspoon freshly ground white pepper
1 quart (4 cups) milk, heated
3 tablespoons Madeira
½ pound lump crabmeat
Salt

Melt butter in medium saucepan over medium-high heat. Add vegetables and sauté until soft. Reduce heat to medium and add flour, whisking constantly until smooth. Cook 5 minutes, whisking frequently. Stir in parsley and seasonings. Gradually add milk, stirring constantly. Add Madeira, crabmeat and salt to taste and simmer 15 to 20 minutes; *do not boil.* Serve hot.

If bisque is thicker than desired, stir in whipping cream to thin.

Cornelia's Clam Chowder

6 to 8 servings

¼ pound salt pork, finely diced
3 medium Bermuda onions, chopped
1 quart clam liquor and/or juice
1½ pounds boiling potatoes, diced

1 pint shucked clams (or more)
1 quart milk

1 4-ounce jar whole pimientos, drained and chopped
1 teaspoon salt
Freshly ground pepper
¾ cup chopped green onion

Butter
Whipping cream or half and half

In a heavy 7- to 9-quart kettle, preferably enameled, fry salt pork on low heat 10 to 15 minutes, until well browned and crisp. Add onion and cook until transparent, about 10 minutes. Pour in clam liquor. Add potato and simmer just below boiling point for 10 minutes.

Meanwhile, put raw clams through meat grinder, food processor or blender, or chop by hand (be careful not to make them into mush!). Stir clams, milk, pimiento, salt and pepper into clam liquor mixture. Cook 15 minutes longer but do not allow to boil. Add green onion for last few minutes of cooking.

Serve in heated bowls with slice of butter and dash of cream.

🍒 *Poultry Cream Soups*

Crème de Volaille Darblay

6 servings

½ cup (1 stick) butter
¾ cup unbleached all purpose flour
6 cups Chicken Broth (see recipe, page 9)
1 cup whipping cream or more to taste
1 teaspoon salt
3 dashes cayenne pepper

1 tablespoon butter
1 cup julienne of carrot
1 cup julienne of leek (white part only)
1 cup julienne of celery
1 cup julienne of turnip

Melt ½ cup butter in large saucepan. Add flour and whisk several minutes to blend. Slowly add stock and bring to boil. Reduce heat and simmer gently 15 minutes. Strain into another saucepan. Stir in cream, salt and cayenne. Soup should lightly coat spoon. Keep warm.

Melt remaining butter in large skillet over medium-high heat. Add vegetable julienne and sauté 1 to 2 minutes; vegetables should still be crunchy. Divide among individual bowls and ladle soup over, or stir vegetables into soup.

2 ❦ Main-Course Soups

Few dishes can match soups for versatility. Although often served as first courses, they also are ideal as main courses for a variety of meals, from a stockpot full of rustic broth and vegetables for the busy parent who needs to feed a hungry family, to a rich legume soup for the vegetarian or simply an elegant fish or meat soup for a romantic candlelit dinner for two.

The best thing about main-course soups, however, is that they are both inexpensive and simple to prepare. Many can be made fully or partially in advance; some benefit from being left for up to two days to allow the flavors to mature. A quick reheating before serving is all that is required. Add good bread, offer a light dessert—perhaps poached fruit or a creamy custard—and you have a meal perfect both for everyday dining and for special occasions.

Many main-course soups border on being stews—traditional one-dish meals with the classic balance of meat, fish or poultry, vegetables and starch. Bourride (page 31), a fennel-scented fish soup ladled over thick croutons and sauced with garlicky Aïoli, is a supper served in the south of France. Chicken, potatoes and corn are the satisfying basics in Ajiaco (page 39), a Colombian favorite; garnished with avocado, cream, hard-cooked eggs and capers and served with a fiery Aji sauce, it makes a spectacular party dish.

Finally, a word about ingredients. As in any type of cooking, main-course soups rely on the best-quality items available: the freshest vegetables and seafood, the most flavorful poultry and beef. Of paramount importance is a good stock. Whenever possible, use a rich meat, poultry or seafood stock of your own creation—simmered for a long time for maximum flavor. You will be rewarded with superb main-course soups that stimulate the palate and comfort the soul.

🍒 *Vegetable Soups*

Basic Puree of Bean Soup with Six Garnishes

A hearty, very simple to prepare soup of dried beans that can be served hot or chilled. Make several batches at once and freeze the extra to serve with different garnishes. For an informal party, offer a selection of garnishes so guests can be creative.

6 servings

6 cups cold water
2 cups dried beans (navy, pea, Great Northern, pinto, broad-beans or soybeans)*
1 slice lemon

¼ cup vegetable oil (preferably cold-pressed safflower)
1 medium-size yellow onion, sliced
1 large carrot, sliced

1 large celery stalk, sliced
1 teaspoon tamari soy sauce

2 cups milk or double-strength reconstituted nonfat dry milk
    Herb or vegetable salt
2 egg yolks
½ cup whipping cream or sour cream
    Garnish (see following recipes)

Combine water, beans and lemon in heavy 4-quart saucepan. Let soak at least 8 hours or overnight.

Discard lemon. Add oil, onion, carrot, celery and soy sauce to undrained beans, adding more water if necessary to cover by 1 inch. Slowly bring to boil over medium heat. Reduce heat, cover and simmer until beans are soft, about 1½ hours. Transfer mixture to processor or blender in batches and puree (or press through fine strainer).

Return puree to saucepan. Blend in milk with herb salt to taste. Combine egg yolks and cream in small bowl. Stir about ½ cup soup into yolk mixture. Add to soup. Place over low and heat through (do not boil). Serve hot or chilled. Garnish as desired.

*Four cups canned chick-peas (garbanzo beans) can be substituted. Do not presoak.

Chopped Tomato and Chives

Use with hot or chilled soup.

2 medium-size ripe tomatoes, peeled, seeded and chopped
    Herb or vegetable salt

¼ cup finely chopped chives or ½ cup chopped green onion

Place tomato in small bowl and sprinkle with salt. Add chives or green onion and toss lightly. Blend into soup and serve.

Chopped Mushrooms and Green Onion

Use with hot soup.

1 tablespoon vegetable oil (preferably cold-pressed safflower)
1 teaspoon fresh lemon juice

1 cup finely chopped mushrooms
    Herb or vegetable salt
½ cup chopped green onion

Heat oil and lemon juice in medium skillet over medium-high heat. Add mushrooms and sauté 1 minute. Season with salt. Stir in green onion. Blend into soup and serve immediately.

Avocado, Onion, Green and Red Pepper

Use with hot or chilled soup.

½ cup finely chopped fresh parsley
1 cup cubed avocado
½ cup chopped white onion

½ cup chopped green bell pepper
½ cup chopped red bell pepper

Stir parsley into soup. Arrange avocado, onion and green and red pepper on serving platter. Pass separately.

Curry and Toasted Nuts

Use with hot or chilled soup.

2 teaspoons curry powder 1 cup finely chopped toasted almonds or peanuts	⅓ cup finely chopped fresh parsley

Stir curry powder into warm soup. Place over low heat and cook (without boiling) about 3 minutes, stirring constantly. Add nuts and parsley.

Spinach and Water Chestnuts

Use with hot soup.

1 cup finely chopped fresh spinach ¾ cup thinly sliced water chestnuts	½ cup freshly grated Parmesan cheese

Add spinach and water chestnuts to soup. Pass cheese separately.

Fines Herbes

Use with hot or chilled soup.

½ cup finely chopped fresh parsley 2 tablespoons finely chopped fresh tarragon or 2 teaspoons dried, crumbled	4 teaspoons finely chopped shallot ¼ teaspoon finely chopped garlic Fried whole wheat croutons for hot soup (optional)

Combine parsley, tarragon, shallot and garlic in small bowl. Sprinkle over each serving. Pass croutons separately.

Soupe au Pistou (Niçoise Vegetable Soup)

6 servings

1 cup plus 1 tablespoon dried Great Northern white beans	5 ounces carrots, halved lengthwise and sliced (about 3 medium)
1 tablespoon olive oil 1 large onion, sliced 2 small leeks, sliced (white and tender green parts) ¼ pound salt pork, trimmed and cut into ¼-inch dice 1½ pounds boiling potatoes, peeled and diced (about 3 large) ½ pound firm zucchini, halved lengthwise and sliced (about 2 small) 6 ounces green beans, cut lengthwise into ½-inch pieces ¼ medium head savoy cabbage, coarsely shredded (about 6 ounces)	1 3-inch square banana squash, peeled and diced 6 cups water ¼ pound frozen lima beans ½ cup elbow macaroni 1 bay leaf ¼ teaspoon dried sage leaf, crumbled Salt and freshly ground pepper 1 cup Pistou (see following recipe) ½ cup freshly grated Parmesan or Romano cheese

Combine beans with enough water to cover in medium saucepan. Let stand overnight. Place undrained beans over medium heat and slowly bring to boil. Reduce heat and simmer 1 hour. Drain.

Heat olive oil in large heavy-bottomed skillet over medium-high heat. Add onion and leek and sauté until wilted. Add salt pork and sauté 5 minutes. Stir in potato, zucchini, green beans, cabbage, carrot and squash. Set aside.

Bring 6 cups water to rapid boil in 12-quart pot over high heat. Reduce heat to medium, add white beans and vegetable mixture and cook 40 minutes.

Add lima beans, macaroni, bay leaf and sage to soup mixture and continue simmering 40 minutes; do not allow macaroni to break up. Season with salt and freshly ground pepper to taste.

Ladle soup into deep bowls. Pass pistou and grated cheese separately.

Pistou

Fragrant with basil and pungent with garlic, this aromatic blend from the south of France will make a simple bowl of soup extraordinary.

Makes 2 cups

2 cups packed fresh basil leaves
½ cup fresh Italian (flat-leafed) or curly parsley leaves
4 garlic cloves
Grated peel of 1 large lemon

¾ cup freshly grated Parmesan or Romano cheese
½ cup olive oil
Salt and freshly ground pepper

With mortar and pestle: Combine basil and parsley in mortar and crush to fine paste. Add garlic and work into paste. Mix in lemon peel. Add cheese and blend well. Gradually stir oil into basil mixture and mix thoroughly; pistou will be consistency of thick mayonnaise. Season with salt and pepper.

With processor: Combine basil, parsley and garlic in work bowl and blend to fine paste, scraping down sides of bowl as necessary. Add lemon peel and cheese and blend well. With machine running, pour oil through feed tube in slow, steady stream and mix well. Season with salt and pepper to taste.

Transfer pistou to jar. Cover surface of pistou with film of olive oil about ⅛ inch thick. Seal jar with tight-fitting lid. Refrigerate for up to 3 months or freeze. Stir oil into pistou before using.

Tomato-Vegetable Soup

The robust tomato base of this soup may be frozen, ready to combine with seasonal vegetables of your choice. Served with freshly baked bread, this makes a wonderful one-course meal.

Flavor and moisture vary in tomatoes during different times of the year and may change texture of base. If too thick, add more stock; if too thin, add uncooked lima beans to pureed base.

6 to 12 servings

3 tablespoons oil
½ cup chopped parsley
2 garlic cloves, minced
1 large onion, sliced
2 ounces ham, chopped
½ teaspoon dried basil
½ teaspoon dried thyme
8 medium tomatoes or 1 28-ounce and 1 15-ounce can Italian plum tomatoes, drained
3 tablespoons tomato paste
4 cups chicken or beef stock or broth
1 teaspoon sugar

Add any of the following:
2 celery stalks, cut into chunks
3 leeks, white part only, coarsely chopped
2 large carrots, sliced

1 large potato, peeled and chopped
1 10-ounce package Italian green beans, thawed
2 small zucchini, sliced
1 cup cauliflower florets
1½ cups baby lima beans or red kidney beans, or combination, partially cooked
1 cup peas
1 small head cabbage, cut into strips, steamed briefly, drained and squeezed dry
½ cup sliced mushrooms
1 pound meatballs (no larger than 1 inch in diameter), cooked and drained
Freshly grated Parmesan cheese (garnish)

Heat oil in Dutch oven or large kettle over medium-high heat. Add next 6 ingredients and sauté until onion is soft and golden. Add tomatoes, tomato paste, stock and sugar. Reduce heat and simmer uncovered 30 minutes. Cool slightly, then place in batches in blender or food processor and puree. Return to pan, taste and add additional seasonings if necessary. *Base may be frozen at this point.*

Add remaining ingredients as desired, starting with those that require longest cooking times, such as potatoes, carrots, cauliflower and lima beans. When partially cooked, add other ingredients. Be careful not to overcook vegetables; they should have a crisp-tender quality. Serve hot, sprinkled with freshly grated Parmesan cheese.

Swiss Beer Soup

This mellow beer-flavored broth topped with a melting layer of Gruyère cheese is a soul-satisfying soup that will take the chill off a crisp fall evening.

4 to 6 servings

1 cup cubed French bread, crusts removed

3 tablespoons oil
1 large onion, chopped
1 garlic clove, minced
12 ounces (1½ cups) beer

3 cups chicken broth*
　Freshly ground pepper
2 tablespoons minced fresh parsley
1½ cups grated Gruyère cheese
1 teaspoon paprika

Preheat oven to 400°F. Arrange bread cubes on baking sheet and toast until golden brown, turning to color evenly.

Preheat broiler. Heat oil in large saucepan over medium heat. Add onion and garlic and sauté until onion is limp and golden. Stir in bread cubes. Add beer and broth and bring to boil. Add pepper and parsley and blend well. Ladle soup into individual heatproof bowls. Divide cheese evenly and sprinkle over soup. Dust with paprika. Run under broiler until cheese is golden brown.

*If using canned chicken broth, add an additional ½ cup water; or use 2 teaspoons bouillon to make 3 cups of broth to avoid the possibility of oversalting.

🍒 Seafood Soups

Bourride (Provençal Fish Soup)

6 servings

　Olive oil
6 ¼-inch-thick slices French bread, cut into rounds to fit bottom of serving bowls

2 tablespoons olive oil
1 medium leek (about 1½ inches in diameter), sliced
1 medium onion, sliced
1 medium carrot, sliced
2 garlic cloves, sliced
½ cup coarsely chopped fresh parsley
1 fennel bulb, coarsely chopped

1 fresh thyme sprig or ½ teaspoon dried, crumbled
2 3-inch strips dried or fresh orange peel
1 bay leaf

3 to 4 pounds assorted fresh bass, cod, flounder and halibut steaks, 1 inch thick
2 cups water
1 cup dry vermouth

5 egg yolks
　Aïoli (see following recipe)

Preheat oven to 350°F. Brush olive oil over bread rounds. Arrange on baking sheet. Bake 4 minutes. Turn bread over and continue baking until toasted, about 4 more minutes. Set aside.

Heat 2 tablespoons olive oil in large, deep, heavy skillet or Dutch oven over medium-high heat. Add leek, onion, carrot, garlic and parsley and sauté until onion is limp. Add fennel, thyme, orange peel and bay leaf and sauté until vegetables are limp, 5 minutes.

Arrange fish over vegetables in skillet in single layer. Pour in water and vermouth. Place over medium-high heat and bring to gentle simmer. Reduce heat to medium, cover partially and poach fish for 9 minutes. Transfer fish to heated platter. Strain broth. Ladle small amount of broth over fish to retain moisture. Cover to keep warm.

Whisk egg yolks with ½ cup Aïoli in heavy saucepan (off heat) until well blended, about 2 to 3 minutes. Whisk in ¼ cup broth 1 drop at a time. Gradually add remaining broth. Place over low heat and cook until sauce is thick enough to coat spoon.

Arrange croutons in heated individual bowls. Divide fish evenly among bowls. Pour sauce over fish and serve immediately. Pass remaining Aïoli separately.

Aïoli (Mediterranean Garlic Mayonnaise)

Splendid as a sauce for fish or poultry, as a dip for crudités, as a dressing for boiled potatoes or as an accompaniment to hard-cooked eggs.

Makes 1⅔ cups

6 garlic cloves
½ teaspoon salt
½ cup fine fresh white breadcrumbs

2 tablespoons fresh lemon juice
2 egg yolks, room temperature
1 cup olive oil

With mortar and pestle: Combine garlic and salt in mortar and crush to paste. Add breadcrumbs and lemon juice and beat until smooth. Blend in egg yolks. Pour olive oil into mixture in slow, steady stream, whisking constantly until thick and creamy. Refrigerate until ready to use.

With processor: Combine garlic and salt in work bowl and blend to fine paste, scraping down sides of bowl as necessary. Add breadcrumbs and lemon juice and process until smooth. Blend in egg yolks. With machine running, pour olive oil through feed tube in slow, steady stream and mix until thick and creamy. Chill until ready to use.

Crab Soup

Makes six 1-cup servings

3 cups half and half
2 cups Béchamel Sauce (see following recipe)
1 10½-ounce can tomato soup
½ cup clam juice
1 pound crabmeat*

6 tablespoons dry Sherry

6 7×7-inch squares puff pastry (pâte feuilletée)

1 egg

Combine first 4 ingredients in heavy-bottomed medium saucepan over low heat. Cook, stirring constantly, until well blended. Add crab and heat through, stirring frequently. Cool, then cover and refrigerate until well chilled.

Divide soup evenly among 6 deep 2-cup soup bowls 4 inches in diameter. Top each with 1 tablespoon Sherry. Transfer bowls to baking sheet and refrigerate until well chilled.

Roll each square of pastry ⅛ inch thick. Cut out 6-inch circles and gently lay over tops of bowls, leaving 1-inch overhang. Seal by pressing firmly to *sides* of bowl (do not crimp to rim; pastry must be allowed to rise freely). Refrigerate until pastry is firm. Cover completely with plastic wrap. Chill overnight.

About 30 minutes before serving, position rack in lower third of oven and preheat to 400°F. Lightly beat egg and use to brush pastry for glaze. Bake until pastry is puffed and golden, about 15 to 20 minutes. Serve immediately.

*If using frozen crab, thaw completely. Rinse, drain and toss with 2 to 3 tablespoons lemon juice before adding to soup.

Béchamel Sauce

Makes 2 cups

3 tablespoons butter
3 tablespoons flour
2 cups milk

½ teaspoon salt
¼ teaspoon freshly ground white pepper

Melt butter in top of double boiler over boiling water. Stir in flour with wooden spoon until smooth. Gradually add milk, stirring constantly, and continue cooking until sauce is thick and smooth. Add salt and pepper. Remove from heat and strain through fine sieve.

Zarzuela Catalana (Spanish Bouillabaisse)

8 to 10 servings

16 mussels in the shell
12 small clams in the shell
Flour

¼ cup olive oil
2 large onions, minced
4 large garlic cloves, minced
1 red pepper, minced
1 green pepper, minced
2 tablespoons minced prosciutto

1 28-ounce can Italian plum tomatoes
¼ teaspoon baking soda
¼ cup Madeira

½ cup blanched almonds, crushed
¼ teaspoon saffron threads, crushed

1 teaspoon sugar
1 teaspoon salt
¼ teaspoon freshly ground pepper
1 bay leaf

2 cups water
1¾ cups dry vermouth or white wine
1 tablespoon fresh lemon juice

16 large unshelled raw shrimp, deveined

½ pound sea scallops, rinsed
1½ pounds cooked lobster or lobster tail, cut into large pieces
8 to 10 Alaska King crab legs
¼ cup Pernod
Rouilleuse (see following recipe)

Scrub mussels and clams, removing all beards and barnacles. Clean by soaking overnight in bucket half-filled with cold water and a handful of flour.

Heat oil in large kettle. Add onion, garlic and green and red pepper and stir-cook for about 5 minutes. Add prosciutto and cook about 1 minute longer.

Halve tomatoes and remove as many seeds as possible. Mash pulp with fork and add with juice to kettle. Add soda (which tempers tartness of tomato) and then Madeira. Bring to boil.

Add almonds, saffron, sugar, salt, pepper and bay leaf and cook until sauce is reduced and thickened, about 30 minutes.

Blend in water, 1½ cups vermouth and lemon juice and cook for 10 minutes. Add shrimp and simmer 5 minutes.

Drain mussels and clams and wash off flour. Put in pan, add remaining ¼ cup vermouth, cover and bring to boil. Steam until shells open. Remove from pan and discard unopened shells. If any grit remains inside shells, rinse under running water; otherwise, add to kettle. Strain cooking liquid through several layers of cheesecloth; add to kettle.

Halve scallops horizontally; add to kettle and cook about 3 minutes.

Just before serving, add lobster and crab legs and heat no more than a minute, just to warm through. Heat Pernod briefly, ignite and pour over seafood. Accompany with Rouilleuse.

Rouilleuse (Red Garlic Mayonnaise)

Makes about 1 cup

4 garlic cloves
2 egg yolks
¼ teaspoon salt
¼ teaspoon red pepper

¼ teaspoon paprika
½ cup olive oil
¼ cup hot zarzuela broth

Mash garlic to pulp in wooden bowl. Add yolks, salt, red pepper and paprika and mix well. Gradually add oil, beating until sauce is consistency of mayonnaise. Slowly stir in hot broth.

Shrimp Chowder

8 to 10 servings

¼ pound bacon, diced
2 tablespoons peanut oil
2 large onions, minced
1 cup diced celery
3 garlic cloves, minced
3 tablespoons flour
1 cup water
2 cups canned plum tomatoes, crushed
1 cup bottled clam juice
6 cups chicken stock

1½ pounds unshelled raw shrimp (15 to 20 per pound)
⅛ teaspoon allspice
⅛ teaspoon ground cloves
⅛ teaspoon saffron threads, crushed

1 bay leaf
Pinch of thyme

2 teaspoons sugar
1 teaspoon filé powder
⅛ teaspoon freshly ground pepper
Dash of hot pepper sauce

½ teaspoon baking soda
2 cups whipping cream
2 tablespoons fresh lime juice or 1 tablespoon fresh lemon juice
1 tablespoon Worcestershire sauce
Dash of red pepper and salt to taste
Minced fresh parsley (garnish)

Sauté bacon in oil until rendered, but do not fry crisp. Transfer bacon to plate. Heat oil and fat; stir in onion, celery and garlic and sauté about 5 minutes. Stir in flour and cook about 1 minute. Add water, tomato, clam juice and stock and bring to boil.

Add shrimp and simmer (*do not boil*) until they just turn pink. Remove shrimp and let cool. Add allspice, cloves, saffron, bay leaf and thyme and continue simmering mixture.

When shrimp are cool enough to handle, shell and devein. Cut each into 3 or 4 pieces and combine with bacon.

Add next 4 ingredients to broth and simmer for about 20 minutes.

Add baking soda (this prevents cream from curdling when added to tomato-broth mixture) and stir well. Add cream, lime or lemon juice, Worcestershire, red pepper and salt and bring just to boil. Add shrimp and bacon and again bring just to boil. Taste and adjust seasoning. Sprinkle with parsley.

Soupe de Poisson au Sauce Rouille
(Fish Soup with Red Garlic Sauce)

8 servings

¼ cup olive oil
4 tomatoes, peeled and chopped
1 medium onion, chopped
1 green pepper, chopped
1 bulb fresh fennel, chopped, or 1 teaspoon dried

2 quarts (8 cups) court bouillon
10 whole black peppercorns
2 bay leaves
1 teaspoon dried thyme
1 teaspoon dried basil
1 teaspoon salt
½ teaspoon saffron

3 pounds thick-fleshed fish (such as halibut, turbot, haddock or red snapper)*

2 cups finely grated Swiss or Parmesan cheese (about ½ pound)

8 7 × 7-inch squares puff pastry (pâte feuilletée)

1 egg
Sauce Rouille (see following recipe)

Heat olive oil in 4- to 5-quart saucepan over medium-high heat. Add next 4 ingredients and sauté until softened.

Add next 7 ingredients, stirring to dissolve saffron. Reduce heat and simmer uncovered for 1 hour, stirring occasionally.

Set strainer over large bowl and line with cheesecloth. Ladle soup through cheesecloth to strain. Cover and chill.

Return soup to saucepan and add fish. Cover with piece of waxed paper and poach gently over low heat until fish is no longer translucent, about 10 to 15 minutes. Remove from heat and let cool to room temperature (or refrigerate if not serving immediately; bring to room temperature before proceeding).

Divide fish evenly among 8 deep 2-cup soup bowls 4 inches in diameter. Ladle poaching liquid into bowls to within about 1 inch of rim. Sprinkle each serving with ¼ cup grated cheese. Transfer bowls to baking sheet and refrigerate until well chilled.

Roll each square of pastry ⅛ inch thick. Cut out 6-inch circles and gently lay over tops of bowls, leaving 1-inch overhang. Seal by pressing firmly to *sides* of bowl (do not crimp to rim; pastry must be allowed to rise freely). Refrigerate until pastry is firm. Cover completely with plastic wrap. Chill overnight.

About 30 minutes before serving, position rack in lower third of oven and preheat to 400°F. Lightly beat egg and use to brush pastry for glaze. Bake until pastry is puffed and golden, 15 to 20 minutes. Serve with Sauce Rouille.

* A combination of 1½ pounds thick-fleshed fish and 1½ pounds seafood (crabmeat, shrimp, clams and/or mussels) may be used for variation. If seafood is precooked, leave in poaching liquid only to heat through.

Sauce Rouille

Makes about 1½ cups

20 croutons or 2 slices bread, toasted and broken into pieces
6 garlic cloves
3 canned pimientos, rinsed and drained

3 egg yolks
2 tablespoons fresh lemon juice
½ teaspoon salt
Pinch of cayenne pepper
1 cup olive oil or peanut oil

Combine all ingredients except oil in processor or blender and mix thoroughly. With machine running, gradually add oil drop by drop until mixture is thickened; remaining oil can be added 1 tablespoon at a time. Continue beating until sauce is consistency of mayonnaise. Transfer to small bowl, cover and chill if not using immediately. Bring to room temperature before serving.

🍎 Fish Stock

As seafood takes on an increasingly important role in the kitchen, so does fish stock (called *fumet* by the French). Seafood dishes hold great appeal for a number of different cooking factions, among them the aficionados of nouvelle cuisine, the health-conscious and those with no time to cook. With a supply of good fish stock in the freezer, the number of seafood recipes in the cook's repertoire multiplies dramatically. It serves as a rich, savory broth for poaching fish and shellfish and as a delectable base for sauces, such as the classic fish *velouté*. It's an indispensable ingredient in many aspics and soups.

Making your own fumet is a simple, speedy process (simmering time is only 35 minutes), once the shopping is completed. A good stock requires absolutely fresh fish bones, trimmings and heads (these contribute body). Since fish markets usually discard these parts right away, it is necessary to order them in advance. Most fish markets will clean the bones and cut them up for a small fee. The best fish to use for this purpose are the lean white varieties—halibut, cod, haddock, sole, pike and flounder—rather than the oily, strong-flavored species, such as mackerel, skate, mullet and bluefish. Salmon can be used, but because it has such a distinctive flavor, any stock made with it should be strictly limited to salmon dishes.

Basic White Wine Fish Stock

Before using for a sauce or soup, boil fish stock and reduce to intensify flavor. Add salt only after reducing stock and combining it with other ingredients

Makes about 1 quart

3 pounds fish bones (heads, frames, trimmings), rinsed, dried and cut into 3-inch pieces	10 parsley sprigs (with stems)
2 tablespoons (¼ stick) butter	6 fresh thyme sprigs or 2 teaspoons dried thyme, crumbled
1 leek (white part only), sliced	½ bay leaf
1 small carrot, sliced	6 white peppercorns, coarsely crushed
1 small celery stalk (with leaves), sliced	3 1½-inch strips lemon peel
2 ounces mushroom stems (optional)	2 cups dry white wine
	5 cups (about) cold water

Discard any feathery red gills from fish heads if necessary (this will prevent stock from tasting bitter). Melt butter in heavy nonaluminum 8-quart pot over low heat. Add fish and next 7 ingredients. Cover and cook, stirring occasionally, until vegetables are translucent, about 10 minutes. Add peppercorns and lemon peel and blend well. Pour in wine and enough water just to cover ingredients (liquids should not be warm or juices will be sealed in rather than extracted). Bring mixture slowly to simmering point. Partially cover pan and reduce heat until liquid is just shaking (do not boil or stock will be cloudy). Cook, skimming foam from surface as necessary, until stock is richly flavored, about 35 minutes.

Line fine sieve or strainer with several layers of dampened cheesecloth and set over large bowl. Strain stock into bowl, pressing down lightly on fish and vegetables with back of spoon to extract as much liquid as possible. Let cool. Refrigerate. Discard fat that accumulates on surface. Store stock in refrigerator, or freeze. If refrigerating, reboil every 3 days to prevent spoilage.
Recipe can be halved or doubled.

Provençal Fish Stock

This zesty stock is the basis for many Mediterranean fish soups and sauces.

Makes about 1 quart

3 pounds fish bones (heads, frames, trimmings), rinsed, dried and cut into 3-inch pieces
2 tablespoons olive oil
1 leek (white part only), sliced
1 small carrot, sliced
1 small celery stalk (with leaves), sliced
2 unpeeled garlic cloves, halved
1 bay leaf
10 parsley sprigs (with stems)
6 fresh thyme sprigs or 2 teaspoons dried thyme, crumbled

3 fresh fennel sprigs or 1 teaspoon fennel seed, crushed
8 white peppercorns, coarsely crushed
3 1½-inch strips orange peel
Pinch of ground red pepper
2 pinches saffron, crushed
1 large tomato, quartered
2 cups dry white wine
¼ cup white wine vinegar
5 cups (about) cold water

Discard any feathery red gills from fish heads if necessary (this will prevent stock from tasting bitter). Heat oil in heavy nonaluminum 8-quart pot over low heat. Add fish and next 8 ingredients. Cover and cook, stirring occasionally, until vegetables are translucent, about 10 minutes. Add peppercorns, orange peel and pepper and blend well. Stir in saffron and tomato. Pour in wine, vinegar and enough water just to cover ingredients. Bring mixture slowly to simmering point. Partially cover pan and reduce heat until liquid is just shaking. Cook, skimming foam from surface as necessary, until stock is richly flavored, about 35 minutes.

Line fine sieve with several layers of dampened cheesecloth and set over large bowl. Strain stock, pressing down lightly with back of spoon to extract liquid. Let cool. Refrigerate. Discard fat from surface. Refrigerate or freeze. If refrigerating, reboil every 3 days to prevent spoilage.

Recipe can be halved or doubled.

Clarified Stock

Clarification removes free-floating particles from stock, leaving it clear and sparkling. To clarify stock, combine 2 egg whites and 1 crushed eggshell in heavy 2-quart saucepan. Gradually whisk in 1 quart of cold, fat-free stock. Place over medium-high heat and stir just until stock reaches a boil. Reduce heat and simmer 15 minutes. Gently ladle stock through fine sieve or strainer lined with dampened dish towel or cheesecloth.

Glace de Poisson (Fish Extract)

This concentrate is used like a bouillon cube. Reconstitute it with water for soup. Boil 1 quart stock in heavy 2-quart saucepan over high heat until reduced to 2 cups, about 30 minutes. Transfer to 1-quart saucepan and boil over medium heat, watching carefully to prevent burning, until reduced to a thick syrupy glaze, about 30 minutes. Remove from heat, cool completely and chill until firm. Cut into teaspoon-size pieces and freeze.

Hungarian Fish Soup à La Mátyás Pince

4 to 6 servings

3 large yellow perch (about 6 pounds total)*
2 quarts water
2 large onions, chopped
2 teaspoons (or more) Hungarian medium-hot paprika

1 small bay leaf
Salt
2 tablespoons sour cream
2 teaspoons fresh lemon juice

Cut heads and tails from fish and place in stockpot or large saucepan. Discard skin from fish; place fish in another large saucepan and set aside. Combine heads and tails with water, half of onion, 2 teaspoons paprika and bay leaf. Bring to boil over high heat. Immediately reduce heat to medium-low and simmer 45 minutes. Strain liquid over fish, pressing solids to extract all liquid. Add remaining onion to fish. Place over medium-low heat and simmer fish 10 minutes per inch of thickness.

Remove fish from pan, using slotted spoon. Discard bones; cut fish into 1-inch chunks. Return to soup. Season to taste with salt and additional paprika, if desired. Place over low heat. Whisk in sour cream and lemon juice. Ladle into bowls and serve immediately.

*If whole perch are not available, substitute 2½ pounds heads, tails and bones of any white-fleshed fish and 3 to 3½ pounds skinned and boned perch fillets.

Regal Fish and Shellfish

Here is a soup that borders on a stew. Pour a fine Chardonnay, accompany with cherry tomatoes and follow with a salad of butter lettuce with oil and vinegar dressing touched with Dijon-style mustard. For dessert: fresh orange tart. If you want to add a first course, try fresh green beans topped with lightly browned butter and finely chopped toasted filberts.

4 servings

1 diced medium onion
1 cup diced leek
½ cup diced celery
6 tablespoons (¾ stick) butter
2 8-ounce bottles clam juice (avoid any dark sediment)
2 cups dry white wine
2 pressed garlic cloves
1 bay leaf
½ teaspoon thyme
¼ teaspoon freshly ground black pepper
Generous dash of Tabasco
⅓ cup finely chopped fresh parsley

12 hard-shell clams in shells, scrubbed
1 pound red snapper (or other rockfish) or sea bass fillets, cut into 1½-inch squares
¾ pound sole fillets, cut into 2½-inch squares
12 medium shrimp, shelled and deveined
1 cup scalded whipping cream
About 20 croutons (garnish) (see following recipe)
Freshly ground white pepper

In a large kettle or Dutch oven over medium heat, sauté onion, leek and celery in butter until very tender. Add clam juice, wine, garlic, bay leaf, thyme, black pepper, Tabasco and ¼ cup parsley. Heat to boiling, then simmer uncovered for 5 minutes.

Add clams and simmer 5 minutes. Add snapper and simmer 3 minutes. Stir in sole and shrimp and simmer 3 minutes more, or until shrimp are pink, clams are open and fish flesh barely separates when tested with a dinner knife. Remove bay leaf. Stir in cream. Ladle into shallow soup plates, arranging shrimp on top. Sprinkle with remaining parsley. Serve croutons and white pepper separately.

Croutons

Slice a French baguette or other slender loaf of French-style bread or French or Italian rolls into slices less than ¼ inch thick. In a large frying pan over medium heat, sauté bread in a generous amount of butter until golden on both sides. Drain on paper towels.

❦ Poultry Soups

Cock-a-Leekie Soup

This soup is good served with warm French bread.

12 servings

2 tablespoons pearl barley*

3 quarts Chicken Broth (see recipe, page 9)

6 leeks, thinly sliced

2½ teaspoons salt

Freshly ground pepper

1 3- to 3½-pound chicken, cooked, skinned, boned and shredded

3 tablespoons chopped fresh parsley

Soften barley by soaking for several hours in enough water just to cover.

Combine undrained barley, stock, leek, salt and pepper in large saucepan and blend well. Cover partially and simmer 1 hour. Add chicken and parsley and simmer another 10 minutes.

*Rice may be substituted for barley. Cook soup for only 30 to 40 minutes before adding shredded chicken and parsley.

Ajiaco

This favorite from Colombia can be prepared in many forms, from simple to elaborate. Our recipe here is for a dish you could serve at a party.

Each diner adds the embellishing ingredients to his own dish according to his taste, helping himself to small scoops of avocado on the side, pouring in cream, sprinkling capers and chopped hard-cooked eggs and spooning on hot and spicy Aji Sauce. Slices of corn can be picked out of the soup and eaten with fingers.

6 servings

1 5-pound roasting chicken, cut into serving pieces
   Water

1 stalk celery with leaves

1 large onion, peeled and quartered

2 bay leaves

1 large parsley sprig

4 tablespoons cumin

2 teaspoons salt

¼ teaspoon freshly ground black pepper

6 medium potatoes, peeled and quartered

6 ears fresh corn

3 ripe avocados, scooped into balls

1 cup whipping cream

½ cup drained capers

4 hard-cooked eggs, chopped
   Aji Sauce (see following recipe)

Cover chicken with cold water. Bring to boil and simmer 5 minutes. Drain liquid and rinse chicken pieces. Return chicken to kettle with 6 cups cold water, celery, onion, bay leaves, parsley, cumin, salt, pepper and 4 peeled and quartered potatoes. Cover, bring to boil and simmer until chicken is tender, about ¾ to 1 hour.

With slotted spoon, remove chicken and potato from broth. Strain broth, removing excess fat from top. Return broth to kettle. Mash cooked potato and stir into broth. Skin and bone chicken, leaving meat in large pieces. Add uncooked potato quarters to broth. Cover kettle and cook until potato is just tender, about 15 minutes.

Cut kernels from 3 ears of corn. Slice remaining corn crosswise into pieces 2 inches thick. When potato is tender, add chicken and all corn to broth. Cook just until corn is tender, about 5 minutes. Taste and correct seasoning with cumin, salt and pepper. Remove bay leaves, if desired. Ladle into wide soup plates, placing a piece of corn and a piece of potato into each. Serve avocado balls on the side. Pass a pitcher of cream and bowls of capers, egg and Aji Sauce.

Aji Sauce

6 tablespoons very finely chopped fresh coriander leaves (if unavailable, use parsley)
½ cup olive oil
2 tablespoons minced green onion (white part only)
1½ tablespoons fresh lemon juice
2 teaspoons finely chopped fresh parsley

1 teaspoon white wine vinegar
½ teaspoon crushed dried hot red peppers (or more for a hotter sauce)
½ teaspoon salt
¼ teaspoon freshly ground black pepper or to taste

Combine all ingredients and mix thoroughly with fork.

Mulligatawny Soup

This classic Anglo-Indian soup, the name of which means "pepper water," should be richly endowed with meat and piquantly spiced. Taste the soup as it cooks, adding lemon juice, cayenne pepper and curry powder as necessary.

12 servings

1 large garlic clove, minced
¼ teaspoon ground cumin seed
6 whole cloves, finely crushed
1 tablespoon curry powder or to taste
¼ teaspoon ground ginger
Cayenne pepper
¼ cup (½ stick) unsalted butter
1 4- to 4¼-pound roasting chicken, cut into serving pieces
Giblets from chicken, coarsely chopped

3 celery stalks with leaves, thinly sliced
2 large onions, chopped
2 carrots, diced

1 leek (white part only), thinly sliced
11 cups (2 quarts plus 3 cups) defatted chicken stock (preferably homemade)
Salt and freshly ground pepper
⅔ cup long-grain rice

2 tart medium apples, peeled, cored and diced
1 cup plain yogurt
2 tablespoons fresh lemon juice or to taste
⅔ cup whipping cream, warmed
Chopped fresh parsley and lightly toasted sliced almonds (garnish)

Combine garlic and spices. Melt butter in large skillet over medium-high heat. Add chicken and sauté until lightly browned on all sides. Add giblets and sauté until cooked through. Transfer chicken and giblets to stockpot.

Drain all but 1 tablespoon fat from skillet. Add celery, onion, carrot, leek and spice mixture and blend well. Add a small ladle of stock and cook over low heat, stirring constantly, until vegetables are tender. Add to chicken. Stir in remaining stock and season with salt and pepper. Cover and simmer 30 minutes. Remove chicken with slotted spoon and set aside. Add rice to soup and continue cooking 15 minutes.

When chicken is cool enough to handle, cut meat into bite-size pieces, discarding skin and bones. Return chicken to soup and blend in apples and yogurt. Simmer 10 minutes. Degrease soup if necessary. Stir in lemon juice, then blend in cream. Taste and adjust seasoning. Pour into heated tureen and sprinkle with parsley and almonds.

Hot and Sour Soup

Serve with green onion pancakes and a crisp Pilsner-style beer.

6 servings

15 dried tiger lily buds*
5 dried Chinese mushrooms*
1 tablespoon dried cloud ears*

7 to 8 cups rich chicken stock
⅓ cup shredded winter bamboo shoots*
½ cup thinly sliced water chestnuts
6 ounces lean pork, finely shredded
4 teaspoons soy sauce
1 20-ounce package tofu (bean curd cake), rinsed and cut into ½-inch dice

1 cup shredded cooked chicken
3 to 5 tablespoons white vinegar
2 to 3 teaspoons freshly ground black pepper
2 tablespoons cornstarch mixed with 3 tablespoons water
1 egg, lightly beaten
1 large green onion, minced (garnish)
Dash of Chinese sesame oil (or more to taste)*

Place tiger lily buds, Chinese mushrooms and cloud ears in separate small bowls and add enough hot water to cover. Soak 30 minutes or until softened. Drain each. Set buds aside. Discard hard centers from cloud ears, then slice remainder into julienne. Remove stems from mushrooms (reserve for later use) and slice caps into julienne.

Combine buds, mushrooms, cloud ears, chicken stock, bamboo shoots, water chestnuts, pork and soy sauce in 5- to 6-quart stockpot and bring to simmer over medium heat. Reduce heat, cover and cook 4 minutes. Add tofu, chicken, vinegar and pepper. Blend in cornstarch mixture and simmer until soup thickens slightly. Stir in beaten egg. Transfer soup to tureen or individual bowls. Sprinkle with green onion and sesame oil and serve.

*Available at oriental markets.

Le Petit Pot à l'Essence de Faisan (Pheasant Soup)

This soup is a specialty of the Hôtel Le Vieux Manoir in Murten, Switzerland, a medieval town considered the country's finest example of a fortified village.

2 servings

1 small pheasant (about 1½ pounds)*
2 cups beef stock (homemade or commercial)
2 cups chicken stock (homemade or commercial)
⅓ cup parsley leaves
1 leek, cut into chunks
1 celery stalk, cut into chunks
1 carrot, cut into chunks
1 small onion, cut into chunks
3 whole black peppercorns

1 sprig fresh sage or ½ teaspoon dried
1 small bay leaf
2 egg whites
½ cup Brunoise (see recipe, page 13)
2 7 × 7-inch squares puff pastry (pâte feuilletée)
1 egg

Combine first 11 ingredients in saucepan and bring to boil. Reduce heat, cover and simmer until pheasant is tender. Cool. Remove pheasant. Refrigerate pheasant and stock separately overnight.

Remove fat from surface of stock and discard. Pour stock into another saucepan, add egg whites and bring slowly to simmer. Continue simmering uncovered over low heat 1 hour; *do not stir.*

Set strainer over large bowl and line with cheesecloth. Ladle soup through cheesecloth to strain. Cover and chill.

Remove meat from pheasant and cut into small dice. Place about ⅓ cup into

2 deep 2-cup soup bowls 4 inches in diameter. Divide Brunoise over meat. Ladle clarified stock into bowls to within about 1 inch of rim. Set bowls on baking sheet and chill well.

Roll each square of pastry ⅛ inch thick. Cut out 6-inch circles and gently lay over tops of bowls, leaving 1-inch overhang. Seal by pressing firmly to *sides* of bowl (do not crimp to rim; pastry must be allowed to rise freely). Refrigerate until pastry is firm. Cover completely with plastic wrap. Chill overnight.

About 30 minutes before serving, position rack in lower third of oven and preheat to 400°F. Lightly beat egg and use to brush pastry for glaze. Bake until pastry is puffed and golden, about 15 to 20 minutes. Serve immediately.

*Duck or game hen can be substituted.

🍎 Meat Soups

Mock Turtle Soup

6 servings

2 pounds top sirloin, well trimmed, cut into small cubes
1 quart (4 cups) beef broth
2 cups chicken broth

½ cup (1 stick) unsalted butter
2 carrots, shredded
2 large onions, cut into wedges ¼ inch thick
½ cup minced celery
2 garlic cloves, pressed or minced
¼ cup flour
1 cup red Bordeaux

½ bay leaf
½ teaspoon marjoram
½ teaspoon summer savory
¼ teaspoon thyme

6 whole allspice
2 whole cloves
¼ cup tomato puree
1 to 3 teaspoons salt (depending on saltiness of broth)
⅛ teaspoon freshly ground pepper
Dash of red pepper
Pinch of saffron threads, crushed
½ cup whipping cream
¼ cup dry Sherry (good quality)
2 tablespoons fresh lemon juice
2 tablespoons finely minced lemon peel
1 tablespoon Worcestershire sauce
¼ teaspoon baking soda
2 tablespoons minced parsley

Combine meat and broths in large kettle. Bring to a boil, then reduce heat and simmer about 1 hour, skimming foam from surface as it collects.

Heat butter in large skillet. Add carrot, onion, celery and garlic and sauté until slightly softened. Stir in flour and cook 1 to 2 minutes. Remove from heat and blend in wine. Add to meat.

Tie next 6 ingredients in cheesecloth bag and add to kettle along with tomato puree. Simmer about 1 hour. Add salt, peppers and saffron and simmer for 1 hour. Blend in remaining ingredients except parsley and simmer about 15 minutes. Taste and adjust seasoning. Stir in parsley. Serve in soup plates.

🍎

Winter Vegetable Borscht

A satisfying soup from the Ukraine. Serve with braided onion-caraway bread and a Pilsner-style beer.

8 to 10 servings

Vegetable oil
4 to 5 pounds meaty beef neck bones, trimmed of fat
1½ pounds beef chuck, trimmed of fat and cut into small cubes

3½ quarts rich beef stock (preferably homemade)
1 bay leaf
Generous pinch *each* of dried thyme and ground cloves

3 tablespoons butter
3 cups chopped onion
2 cups diced rutabaga

1 cup diced carrot
3 cups chopped cabbage
3 cups chopped beet
1 teaspoon sugar
Pinch of freshly grated nutmeg

Salt and freshly ground pepper
½ cup fresh lemon juice
2 tablespoons minced flat-leaf (Italian) parsley (garnish)
3 tablespoons minced fresh dillweed or 1 tablespoon dried (garnish)
2 cups sour cream

Preheat broiler. Generously oil large, shallow pan. Arrange bones and meat in pan in single layer. Broil as close to heat source as possible, turning to brown all sides, about 10 minutes.

Transfer meat and bones to 6- to 8-quart saucepan. Add beef stock, bay leaf, thyme and cloves. Cover partially and bring to simmer. Simmer over medium-low heat about 2 hours. Transfer bones to platter, using slotted spoon. Trim off all meat. Return meat to saucepan (discard bones). Skim off as much fat as possible from surface.

Melt butter in large skillet over medium-high heat. Add onion, rutabaga and carrot. Cook, stirring frequently, until onion begins to color. Add to soup stock with cabbage, beet, sugar and nutmeg. Cover and simmer until vegetables are tender, about 30 minutes. *(Soup can be prepared ahead to this point and refrigerated overnight.)*

Just before serving, reheat soup if necessary. Season with salt and pepper to taste. Stir in lemon juice. Transfer soup to tureen or individual bowls. Garnish with parsley and dillweed. Pass sour cream separately.

Cream of Reuben Soup

8 generous servings

½ cup beef broth
½ cup chicken broth
¼ cup coarsely chopped celery
¼ cup coarsely chopped onion
¼ cup coarsely chopped green pepper
1 tablespoon cornstarch dissolved in 2 tablespoons water
1 cup coarsely chopped corned beef (about ¼ pound)

1 cup chopped Swiss cheese
¾ cup sauerkraut, drained and rinsed

¼ cup (½ stick) butter
2 cups half and half
Chopped fresh chives (garnish)

Combine first 5 ingredients in large saucepan and bring to boil over high heat. Reduce heat and simmer until vegetables are crisp-tender, about 5 minutes. Add dissolved cornstarch and continue cooking until soup thickens. Remove from heat and stir in corned beef, Swiss cheese and sauerkraut, blending well.

Melt butter in large double boiler over medium heat. Stir in half and half. Add soup and blend until smooth. Heat through but do not boil. Garnish with chopped fresh chives.

🍎 Brown Stock

Whenever a sauce or soup has particularly good flavor, its quality may well be credited to the stock used to make it. One of the most useful is brown stock, a savory liquid made from the slow simmering of browned veal or beef, vegetables, seasonings and water. It provides the flavor base for innumerable soups, sauces, stews and vegetable dishes. When cooked down until most of the liquid has evaporated, brown sauce becomes *glace de viande,* a potent beef concentrate (1 teaspoon of glace de viande combined with 1 quart water makes 1 quart beef stock).

It is important to make brown stock from only the best ingredients available. Use the tougher, more flavorful cuts of meat. Bones and vegetables must be fresh. Even the water should be pure and free from off flavors. The stock may leave its signature on a dozen meals; it should be the best you can make.

Brown Stock

Makes 5 to 6 cups

3 tablespoons oil	4 garlic cloves, unpeeled and lightly crushed
3 pounds veal or beef shank or other veal or beef cut with bones	2 bay leaves
3 pounds bottom round, chuck, sirloin or other lean stewing beef	1 teaspoon black peppercorns
3 medium carrots, sliced	3 sprigs parsley
3 celery stalks, including leaves, cut into 2-inch pieces	½ teaspoon thyme
1 large onion, quartered	4 to 5 quarts water (preferably purified drinking water)
1 large onion, peeled, studded with 4 whole cloves	

Preheat oven to 375°F. Pour oil into large, shallow roasting pan. Place bones and meat in pan, turning to coat with oil. Roast uncovered 30 minutes.

Add remaining ingredients except water. Roast an additional 30 minutes. Transfer meat and vegetables to a 12- to 16-quart stockpot. Add 1 quart water to roasting pan. Bring to boil over high heat, scraping brown bits from bottom and sides of pan. Pour contents of roasting pan into stockpot and add enough water to cover meat and bones, about 3 to 4 quarts. Place uncovered over medium heat and bring slowly to a boil, about 30 minutes. (Slow heating helps extract juices from meat, making a more flavorful stock. If water is brought too rapidly to a boil, nutrients and flavor will be sealed in rather than released into the stock.) Reduce heat and simmer uncovered 8 hours. Skim off film as it rises to the surface.

Remove meat and vegetables with slotted spoon. Strain stock through fine sieve. Refrigerate several hours or overnight. When stock is cold, remove solidified fat from surface.

Variations

Glace de viande (Meat Glaze)

Glace de viande will keep in the refrigerator for several months in a tightly closed jar. If molding should occur, wash away with hot water—glace de viande is still good. It can also be frozen: place teaspoonfuls into small plastic bags and defrost as needed.

Place 1 quart brown stock in a 2-quart saucepan. Cook uncovered over medium heat 1 to 1½ hours. As it reduces, transfer it to successively smaller saucepans; this lessens the chance of burning glaze. As stock is reduced, it will become syrupy and coat the back of a metal spoon. When allowed to stand, it will solidify.

Clarified Brown Stock

1 quart cold, fat-free stock	1 eggshell, crushed
1 egg white, lightly beaten	

Combine all ingredients in 2-quart saucepan. Stir over low heat just until stock boils. Cook uncovered over very low heat 20 minutes. Let stand 15 minutes. Strain stock through a colander lined with several layers of dampened cheesecloth.

Consommé Double

Follow directions for clarified stock, adding 1 pound lean ground beef. Cook 1 hour. Chill completely, then degrease.

Great Hints

- Add a tablespoon of cold water to simmering stock; this causes more film to rise to the surface and decreases the number of times you will need to skim.
- Do not use pork, lamb or starchy vegetables such as potatoes to make brown stock.
- Salt is not used in the preparation of brown stock because salt does not cook away along with the liquid. Plan on salting to taste when using stock in other dishes.
- Stock will keep in refrigerator a minimum of 3 days. After 3 days, either bring to boil and rechill or freeze in batches. An empty milk carton is a good freezer container.

Beef in Brandy Broth

Serve this thick soup-stew with crusty French bread and a nice round Burgundy. Follow with a green salad and, if you wish, a cheese course. Finish with a tart of caramelized pears or a tarte tatin, *made with caramelized apples.*

5 to 6 servings

3 pounds beef chuck, cut into 1½-inch cubes
Salt and freshly ground black pepper
6 tablespoons (¾ stick) butter
1 6 × 1-inch strip orange zest
12 to 15 small boiling onions, peeled
⅔ cup very strong beef stock or undiluted condensed beef broth

½ cup brandy
1 large garlic clove, pressed
6 carrots, peeled and cut into 2 × ¼-inch strips
4 teaspoons grated fresh lemon peel
4 tablespoons finely chopped fresh parsley

Blot meat with paper towels. Season with salt and sprinkle generously with pepper. Heat butter in large heavy kettle or Dutch oven over medium heat until it bubbles and begins to brown. Add meat, turning to coat each piece with butter. Add orange zest. Arrange onions over meat.

Stir together stock, ¼ cup brandy and garlic. Add to meat. Cover and cook without stirring over very low heat about 2½ hours or until meat is tender. Add carrot strips, tucking them beneath liquid. Cover and simmer just until tender, about 30 minutes. Gently stir in lemon peel, remaining ¼ cup brandy and 2 tablespoons parsley. Taste and add more salt, if necessary. Ladle into shallow soup plates. Sprinkle with remaining parsley.

Goulash Soup with Sauerkraut

This soup mellows and improves in flavor if prepared a day in advance. Serve with dark bread and either robust Hungarian Egri Bikavér or a tart dark beer.

6 to 8 servings

1 tablespoon vegetable oil
1½ to 2 pounds lean pork, cut into ½-inch cubes

3 to 4 tablespoons butter or lard
4 large onions, finely chopped
4 carrots, finely chopped
2 celery stalks, finely chopped
1 large garlic clove, minced
2 to 3 tablespoons imported Hungarian sweet paprika
1½ teaspoons fresh thyme or ½ teaspoon dried, crumbled
1½ teaspoons fresh savory or ½ teaspoon dried, crumbled

¼ teaspoon whole caraway seed
2½ to 3 quarts beef stock (preferably homemade)
2 cups canned tomatoes in puree
1 cup chopped cabbage
1 pound sauerkraut, rinsed and drained
2 large potatoes, peeled and cut into small cubes
Salt and freshly ground pepper
Sour cream (optional garnish)

Preheat broiler. Lightly coat shallow baking pan with 1 tablespoon oil. Add pork in single layer. Broil quickly until well browned on all sides. Drain thoroughly on paper towels.

Melt butter or lard in 6- to 8-quart saucepan over medium-high heat. Add onion, carrot and celery and cook until onion begins to brown. Stir in pork, garlic, paprika, thyme, savory and caraway. Add stock, tomatoes and cabbage. Reduce heat, cover partially and simmer about 1½ hours. Stir in sauerkraut and simmer 30 minutes. Add potato and simmer another 30 minutes. Season with salt and pepper. Transfer soup to tureen or individual bowls. Serve immediately. Garnish with dollop of sour cream, if desired.

Spicy Sausage and Clam Soup

Serve with hot, crusty bread.

6 to 8 servings

¼ cup olive oil
1 pound hot Italian sausage, casings removed
1 pound fresh mushrooms, coarsely chopped
2 cups sliced onion (about 2 medium onions)
1 28-ounce can whole peeled Italian tomatoes, undrained

1 cup dry white wine
1 cup fresh or bottled clam juice
2 tablespoons fresh basil or 2 teaspoons dried, crumbled
1 tablespoon minced garlic

1 large bunch parsley, chopped
6 dozen littleneck clams, scrubbed

Heat olive oil in large Dutch oven or flameproof casserole over medium heat. Add sausage, mushrooms and onion and cook, stirring frequently and breaking up sausage with fork, until sausage loses pink color, about 10 minutes. Stir in tomatoes. Bring mixture to boil, crushing tomatoes into small pieces. Reduce heat to low and simmer 5 minutes. Pour in wine and clam juice. Return mixture to boil. Reduce heat to low, cover and simmer 20 minutes, stirring occasionally. Add basil and garlic and cook 5 minutes longer. (*Stock can be prepared 1 day ahead to this point, covered and refrigerated until ready to use.*)

Before serving, transfer stock to pot large enough to accommodate stock and clams. Bring to boil over high heat. Reserve half of parsley for garnish and add remaining parsley to pot. Add clams. Reduce heat to medium-high, cover and simmer until clams open, about 5 to 10 minutes; *discard any clams that do not open.* Ladle soup into bowls and sprinkle with reserved parsley. Serve immediately.

If large stockpot is not available, use two pots and divide ingredients evenly.

China Honey Pork and Greens

This soup goes well with a California Zinfandel and sliced cold, fresh oranges garnished with feathers of Chinese parsley (also called cilantro or coriander). It should be served with individual bowls of additional rice. A fresh apple-nut torte with whipped cream or a date-nut or pecan-and-cream-layered meringue torte completes the meal.

6 servings

1 3-pound fresh boneless pork shoulder blade or butt (about 3½ pounds before boning and tying)

3 tablespoons honey

2 tablespoons peanut oil
6 cups cold water
1 cup dry white wine
3 tablespoons sugar
⅛ teaspoon crushed dried hot red peppers

¼ cup soy sauce
½ teaspoon freshly ground white pepper

3 pounds bok choy (Chinese cabbage)
1½ cups hot steamed white rice
Additional soy sauce and freshly ground white pepper

Place meat in large heavy kettle or Dutch oven and cover with cold water. Heat to boiling, then cover and simmer 1 hour. Drain off water and dry meat. Rub roast with honey.

Heat oil in kettle over medium heat. Add meat and brown well on all sides. Add water, wine, sugar, red peppers, soy sauce and white pepper. Cover tightly and simmer about 2 hours or until meat is *very* tender, turning occasionally. Place meat on plate and remove strings. Keep meat warm.

Trim off and discard solid ends of cabbage. Cut remaining cabbage (about 2 pounds) crosswise, slicing tender top portions into 1½-inch pieces and heavy lower portions into 1-inch pieces. Heat liquid in kettle to boiling. Add greens and cook just until tender, about 5 to 10 minutes. Serve a portion of meat, some greens, a spoonful of rice and a ladleful of broth in each soup bowl. Pass soy sauce and white pepper.

Spanish Sausage and Lentil Soup

This soup is even better the second or third day after preparation. Serve with egg bread and a full-bodied Spanish Rioja or California Barbera.

8 to 10 servings

2 tablespoons olive oil
1 pound chorizo or other spicy garlic sausage
7 ounces smoked ham, finely chopped
2 large onions, finely chopped
1 large green pepper, seeded and finely chopped
1 medium carrot, finely chopped
2 garlic cloves, minced
1 bay leaf
¾ teaspoon fresh thyme or ¼ teaspoon dried, crumbled

½ teaspoon whole cumin seed, ground

8 to 9 cups rich chicken stock (preferably homemade)
1 1-pound can peeled tomatoes
½ pound dried lentils (1¼ cups)

Salt and freshly ground pepper
12 large spinach leaves, washed, trimmed and finely shredded

Heat olive oil in heavy 6- to 8-quart saucepan over medium heat. Add sausage and cook until almost all fat is rendered. Transfer sausage to platter. Drain off all but 2 tablespoons grease from saucepan. Add ham, onion, green pepper and carrot to saucepan. Cover and cook 15 minutes, stirring occasionally. Stir in garlic, bay leaf, thyme and cumin. Cover and cook another 5 minutes.

Meanwhile, thinly slice sausage. Add to saucepan with chicken stock, tomatoes and lentils. Reduce heat to low, cover partially and simmer gently until lentils begin to dissolve, about 2 hours. *(Can be prepared up to 3 days ahead to this point and refrigerated, or frozen up to 3 months.)*

Discard any fat from surface. Taste and adjust seasoning with salt and freshly ground pepper. Simmer just until warmed through. Add shredded spinach. Transfer soup to tureen or individual bowls and serve immediately.

3 🍎 Cold Soups

For all their rich taste and icy tang, the *real* secret behind the popularity of cold soups is elegance without fuss. Unlike their long-simmered hot counterparts, most cold soups can be whipped up in a matter of minutes, often with just a blender or food processor. Chopping, mincing and dicing are kept to a minimum, and fresh vegetables often replace time-consuming stocks to lend body and flavor. Best of all, busy cooks know that most cold soups benefit from advance preparation, which allows the mixtures to develop their fullest flavor.

Although cold soups are natural warm-weather companies, their appeal isn't limited by the season. A beautifully vivid cold soup, such as the Iced Parsley Soup on page 53 or the Chilled Ginger-Carrot Soup on page 51, can be served in a clear glass bowl for a glamorous beginning to lunch or dinner any time of the year. And many soups, including delicate Artichoke Soup (page 50) garnished with a smooth white custard, classic Vichyssoise (page 52) and fresh-tasting Asparagus Soup (page 51), can be served either hot or cold as the mood dictates.

Another advantage of cold soups is their portability. Turn a weekend picnic into an event with a vacuum bottle filled with Cold Mint-Cucumber Soup (page 52), spicy Gazpacho Blanco (page 52) or Curried Cream of Pea Soup (page 54). Crisply cooked bacon adds a delightful smoky nuance to Cold Zucchini Soup (page 55), which is finished with a hint of Sherry.

Chilled fruit soups are a particularly versatile component of the cook's repertoire. Iced Cantaloupe Soup (page 56) spiced with cardamom is an ideal first course, but the Soup of Peaches and Mint (page 56)—scoops of homemade mint sorbet topped with pureed and sliced peaches, then garnished with fresh berries and a creamy almond jelly—proves that cold fruit soups make striking and unusual desserts as well.

🍎 *Vegetable Soups*

Artichoke Soup

Serve hot or chilled.

6 servings

¼ cup vegetable oil (preferably cold-pressed safflower)

2 tablespoons finely chopped shallot
Freshly ground white pepper

2 tablespoons rice flour or all purpose flour (preferably unbleached)

3 cups chicken or vegetable stock

2 7½-ounce cans artichoke bottoms, sliced (reserve 2 whole bottoms)

1 teaspoon fresh lemon juice

2 tablespoons (¼ stick) unsalted butter

¾ cup double-strength reconstituted nonfat dry milk or half and half
Herb or vegetable salt

½ cup whipping cream, whipped

2 teaspoons finely grated lemon peel

2 teaspoons finely chopped fresh parsley
White Custard (optional garnish) (see following recipe)

Heat oil in heavy 3-quart saucepan over low heat. Add shallot and season with pepper. Cook 2 minutes. Remove from heat and stir in flour. Place over medium heat, add stock and bring to boil, stirring constantly. Add sliced artichoke bottoms and lemon juice. Reduce heat and simmer 30 minutes.

Transfer mixture to processor or blender in batches and puree (or press through fine strainer). Return puree to saucepan. Place over low heat. Stir in butter a little at a time. Blend in milk or half and half and season to taste with herb salt. Thinly slice remaining artichoke bottoms and add to soup. Fold in whipped cream. Combine lemon peel and parsley in small dish. Ladle soup into bowls. Top each serving with some of White Custard, if desired, and sprinkle lightly with lemon peel mixture.

White Custard

½ cup milk or double-strength reconstituted nonfat dry milk
Sea or coarse salt

Freshly ground white pepper

2 egg whites

Oil 8-inch square cake pan. Preheat oven to 300°F. Bring milk, salt and pepper to boil slowly in small saucepan over medium heat. Remove from heat and let cool. In small bowl set over larger bowl of ice cubes, whisk egg whites lightly (do not beat until foamy). Add scalded milk little by little, stirring after each addition. Pour into prepared cake pan. Bake until custard is firm, about 15 minutes. Cool in refrigerator. Turn custard out onto work surface and cut into very small squares.

🍎

Asparagus Soup

Serve hot or chilled.

4 servings

3 tablespoons vegetable oil (preferably cold-pressed safflower)
24 fresh asparagus spears (tips reserved), sliced
1 cup chopped green onion
1 teaspoon fresh lemon juice
½ teaspoon finely chopped garlic
Freshly ground white pepper
1 tablespoon whole wheat pastry flour
2 cups water

½ cup double-strength reconstituted nonfat dry milk or whipping cream
1 egg yolk
2 tablespoons chopped fresh parsley
Herb or vegetable salt

Heat oil in heavy 4-quart saucepan over low heat. Add asparagus (excluding tips), green onion, lemon juice and garlic. Cover and cook until asparagus is crisp-tender, about 5 to 10 minutes. Season with pepper. Remove from heat and stir in flour. Place over low heat, add water and bring to boil, stirring constantly. Reduce heat to very low and simmer 10 minutes. Transfer mixture to processor or blender in batches and puree (or press through fine strainer). Return puree to saucepan and set aside.

Cook asparagus tips in large saucepan of boiling water until crisp-tender, about 5 minutes. Drain well; add to soup. Stir in milk or cream.

Combine egg yolk with ½ cup soup in small bowl. Add yolk mixture to soup. Stir in parsley. Place over low and heat through; do not boil. Season to taste with herb or vegetable salt.

Chilled Ginger-Carrot Soup

4 servings

¼ cup (½ stick) butter
⅓ cup chopped green onion
3 cups sliced carrot
1 teaspoon sugar
½ teaspoon ground ginger
¼ teaspoon cinnamon
1 tablespoon all purpose flour
½ teaspoon salt

¼ teaspoon freshly ground white pepper
2 cups water
1½ cups fresh orange juice
½ cup whipping cream
1 teaspoon fresh lemon juice
Orange slices or carrot julienne (garnish)

Melt butter in large heavy saucepan over medium heat. Add green onion and sauté until tender, about 3 to 4 minutes. Stir in carrot, sugar, ginger and cinnamon and sauté 3 more minutes. Blend in flour, salt and pepper and toss until carrot slices are coated with flour. Cook 1 minute. Add water and orange juice and bring to boil. Reduce heat to medium-low, cover and simmer until carrot is tender, about 20 minutes. Cool slightly. Transfer mixture to processor or blender in batches and puree until smooth. Pour into large bowl. Stir in whipping cream and lemon juice. Taste and adjust seasoning. Cover and refrigerate several hours or overnight. To serve, ladle into bowls and garnish with orange slices or carrot julienne.

Cold Mint-Cucumber Soup

This delicate and unusual combination is refreshing on a hot day.

4 to 6 servings

3 tablespoons butter
1 medium onion, finely chopped
1 small garlic clove, minced
3 medium cucumbers, peeled and thinly sliced
3 tablespoons flour (preferably rice flour)
2 cups chicken stock

2 tablespoons finely chopped fresh mint
1 cup half and half
1 cup plain yogurt
Salt and freshly ground white pepper
Sliced cucumber (garnish)

Melt butter in large skillet over medium heat. Add onion and garlic and sauté until limp but not brown. Add sliced cucumber and cook slowly until soft. Remove from heat. Stir in flour, then stock, blending well. Place over medium-high heat and bring to boil. Reduce heat and simmer 5 minutes. Transfer to processor or blender in batches and puree. Pour into bowl and blend in mint. Cover and chill well. Just before serving, stir in half and half and yogurt and mix well. Taste and season with salt and pepper. Garnish each serving with sliced cucumber.

Gazpacho Blanco

2 servings

1 cucumber, peeled, seeded and cut into chunks
½ cup chicken broth
½ cup sour cream or plain yogurt
1 small garlic clove, chopped
2 to 3 teaspoons white wine vinegar or to taste
Salt

Garnish
Chopped tomato
Chopped green onion

Combine all ingredients except garnish in processor or blender and mix until smooth. Pour into serving bowls. Sprinkle with chopped tomato and green onion before serving.

Leek Soup (Vichyssoise)

May be served hot or cold.

6 servings

3 cups diced potato
3 cups thinly sliced leek (2 large leeks)
2 quarts water
1 tablespoon salt
1 teaspoon basil
½ teaspoon white pepper

6 tablespoons whipping cream
3 tablespoons butter, room temperature
Parsley or chives (garnish)

Combine vegetables with water, salt, basil and pepper in large saucepan and simmer until tender, about 40 to 50 minutes. Puree in blender or food mill.

To serve hot, add whipping cream and butter. Omit butter if serving chilled. Garnish with parsley or chives.

One-half cup carrots and/or celery may also be added, if desired.

Cold Lentil Soup

4 servings

2 cups dried lentils

4 cups beef stock
1 small ham hock
3 garlic cloves
2 celery stalks, chopped

½ teaspoon ground cumin
½ cup plain yogurt or sour cream
3 tablespoons curry powder or to taste

Soak lentils in large saucepan in enough water to cover for 30 minutes. Drain well. Cover with fresh water and bring to full boil. Reduce heat and simmer for 10 minutes. Drain again.

Combine lentils with stock, ham hock, garlic, celery and cumin. Place over medium-high heat and bring to boil. Reduce heat and simmer 2 hours, stirring occasionally. Discard ham. Puree soup in batches in processor or blender. Transfer to bowl. Combine yogurt or sour cream with curry powder. Stir into puree, blending thoroughly. Cover and chill well. Stir again before serving.

Cold Olive Soup

Makes about 1 quart

1 pint (2 cups) plain yogurt
1 10½-ounce can chicken broth
1 cup thinly sliced pitted black olives
½ cup chopped peeled cucumber

¼ cup diced green onion
¼ cup diced green pepper
1 tablespoon minced fresh parsley
Freshly ground pepper
Sliced black olives (garnish)

Combine all ingredients except garnish in large mixing bowl and blend well. Chill overnight. To serve, ladle into bowls and garnish with remaining olives.

Iced Parsley Soup

6 to 8 servings

3 large leeks (including 3 inches of greens), slit lengthwise

2 tablespoons (¼ stick) unsalted butter
6 cups chicken stock
3 medium potatoes, peeled and cubed
Salt and freshly ground white pepper

1 large bunch fresh Italian parsley (stems removed), chopped

1 cup whipping cream
Freshly ground pepper
2 tablespoons minced fresh parsley (garnish)

Wash leeks thoroughly in cold water. Transfer to bowl, cover with ice cold water and let stand 30 minutes.

Drain leeks well; slice thinly. Melt butter in heavy large saucepan over medium heat. Add leek and ¼ cup stock. Cover and cook until leek is soft. Add potato cubes and remaining chicken stock and bring to boil. Taste and season with salt and pepper. Reduce heat, cover and simmer until potato is quite soft, about 30 minutes. Add chopped parsley and simmer for an additional 10 minutes.

Puree soup in batches in processor or blender, transferring to large bowl as it is pureed. Blend in cream. Taste and adjust seasoning. Cover and chill until serving time. Garnish each serving with a generous grinding of pepper and a sprinkling of minced parsley.

Curried Cream of Pea Soup

6 servings

1 cup shelled fresh or frozen peas
1 medium onion, sliced
1 carrot, sliced
1 celery stalk (with leaves), sliced
1 medium potato, peeled and sliced

1 garlic clove
1 teaspoon curry powder or to taste
  Salt and freshly ground pepper
2 cups chicken stock
1 cup half and half

Combine vegetables and seasonings with 1 cup stock in saucepan. Bring to boil; reduce heat, cover and simmer 15 minutes. Puree in batches in processor or blender. Pour into bowl and whisk in remaining stock and half and half. Serve chilled or at room temperature.

Avgolemono Soup

Serve chilled or at room temperature.

2 servings

2 cups light chicken broth
2 tablespoons long-grain rice
1 egg

4½ teaspoons fresh lemon juice
  Salt
2 thin lemon slices (garnish)

Combine chicken broth and rice in medium saucepan and bring to boil over high heat. Reduce heat to low, cover and simmer until rice is just tender, about 15 to 20 minutes. Remove from heat. Beat egg in small bowl until fluffy and pale yellow. Beat in lemon juice. Slowly whisk about ⅔ cup hot broth into egg mixture, then whisk back into remaining broth. Remove from heat and continue whisking until slightly thickened. Let cool, then chill. Just before serving, stir through several times and add salt to taste. Garnish with lemon slices.

Tomato and Coriander Soup

Fresh coriander (called Chinese parsley in this country and cilantro in Mexico and South America) is a strongly flavored herb that resembles parsley. Used sparingly, it is a particularly good way to perk up a fresh tomato soup.

4 to 6 servings

2 tablespoons (¼ stick) butter
½ cup finely diced celery
3 large shallots, finely minced
2 large garlic cloves, finely minced
2 tablespoons finely minced fresh oregano or 1 teaspoon dried
2 tablespoons finely minced fresh parsley
2 tablespoons finely minced fresh coriander
3 pounds large ripe tomatoes, peeled, seeded and chopped

1 tablespoon tomato paste
1 bay leaf
  Salt and freshly ground pepper
4 cups chicken stock or bouillon

4 tablespoons full-bodied olive oil
1 small zucchini, diced

2 tablespoons flour
  Crème fraîche or sour cream (garnish)

Melt butter in large heavy saucepan over low heat. Add next 6 ingredients, cover partially and cook until mixture is soft but not browned, about 5 to 8 minutes. Add tomato, tomato paste, bay leaf, salt and pepper. Increase heat and bring to boil. Stir in stock. Reduce heat, cover partially and simmer 45 minutes. Remove from heat and let cool. Puree in batches in processor or blender. Set aside in mixing bowl.

Heat 2 tablespoons olive oil in small skillet over medium-high heat. Add zucchini and sauté until nicely browned on all sides. Remove from heat.

Heat remaining oil in small pan over medium heat. Whisk in flour and stir constantly until roux is smooth and hazelnut brown in color. Add to puree, blending well. Stir in zucchini. Serve chilled or at room temperature; if serving chilled, thin with additional stock if necessary. Garnish each serving with a dollop of crème fraîche or sour cream.

Chilled Fresh Tomato Soup

4 servings

2 tablespoons olive oil
1 medium onion, sliced
1 medium carrot, sliced
⅓ cup chopped fresh parsley
2 garlic cloves, mashed
4 large ripe tomatoes, peeled, cored and chopped

1 sprig fresh thyme
1 sprig fresh basil
1 teaspoon salt
2 cups vegetable stock
   Lemon or lime wedges

Heat oil in medium saucepan over medium-high heat. Add onion, carrot, parsley and garlic and sauté until well softened. Transfer to food processor or blender with tomato, herbs and salt; puree. Add vegetable stock and mix well. Cover and chill thoroughly. Serve with lemon or lime wedges.

Puree can be put through wire strainer for a soup with smoother consistency.

Cold Zucchini Soup

4 servings

3 pounds unpeeled zucchini, coarsely chopped
4 cups (or more) chicken stock
5 slices bacon, chopped, cooked crisp and drained
⅓ cup minced fresh parsley

1 garlic clove, pressed
1½ teaspoons dried basil
   Salt and freshly ground white pepper
   Paprika (garnish)
4 teaspoons dry Sherry (optional)

Combine all ingredients except paprika and Sherry in saucepan and bring to boil. Reduce heat and simmer until zucchini is tender, about 15 minutes. Transfer to processor or blender in batches and puree, adding more stock if mixture seems too thick (it will thicken as it cools). Pour into bowl and let cool. Cover and chill well. Ladle into individual bowls and sprinkle with paprika. Stir Sherry into each serving if desired.

🍎 Dessert Soups

Iced Cantaloupe Soup

6 to 8 servings

2 ripe large cantaloupes, peeled, seeded and coarsely chopped
1½ cups dry Sherry
2 tablespoons fresh lime juice
2 tablespoons whipping cream
Large pinch of sugar
⅛ teaspoon cardamom
Blueberries or kiwi slices (garnish)

Combine all ingredients except garnish in processor or blender (in batches if necessary) and puree until very smooth. Refrigerate at least 2 hours. Serve in chilled bowls. Garnish with blueberries or kiwi.

Soupe de Pêches à la Menthe (Soup of Peaches and Mint)

6 servings

Mint Sorbet
2¼ pounds (4⅔ cups) sugar
10 cups water
10 fresh mint sprigs

Almond Jelly
1 cup milk
¼ teaspoon almond extract
¼ cup sugar
1 tablespoon unflavored gelatin

Peaches
12 fresh peaches or 2 29-ounce cans sliced Elbertas, drained, rinsed and patted dry

6 tablespoons kirsch
Juice of 2 oranges (about ½ cup)
2 tablespoons honey

Whole strawberries, raspberries and mint sprigs (garnish)
6 cinnamon sticks (optional garnish)

For sorbet: Bring sugar and water to boil in pot. Remove from heat and add mint; cover and let steep 5 to 10 minutes. Strain. Freeze in ice cream maker according to manufacturer's directions or turn into metal pan and place in freezer until solid.

Partially thaw sorbet, then beat in processor until smooth and fluffy. Turn into airtight plastic container and refreeze until ready to serve. *(Sorbet is best if served within 24 hours.)*

For jelly: Heat milk and extract in small saucepan. Add sugar and gelatin and heat briefly until gelatin is completely dissolved. Strain into 8-inch glass baking pan and chill thoroughly.

For peaches: Peel, halve and pit 6 peaches (or use 1 can). Puree in processor, adding kirsch gradually. Peel and slice remaining peaches and mix with orange juice and honey. Chill.

To serve, dice almond jelly. Scoop sorbet into serving bowls. Pour peach puree over, then top with sliced peaches. Garnish with diced jelly, whole strawberries, raspberries, mint sprigs and, if desired, cinnamon sticks.

Spicy Italian Sausage and Clam Soup;
Green Bean, Walnut and Feta Salad

Zarzuela Catalana (Spanish Bouillabaisse)

Nona's Salad Egg Drop Soup (right);
Spanish Sausage and Lentil Soup (far right)

Dan Wolfe

Ajiaco

Goulash Soup with Sauerkraut

4 ❦ Appetizer and Side Salads

Beyond the classic combination of lettuce, tomato and simple vinaigrette dressing, which probably appears on the dinner table more than any other appetizer or accompaniment, salads come in many guises. Ranging from the everyday, like the Carrot and Parsnip Salad on page 60, to the decidedly elegant, such as Soufflé-Stuffed Artichokes (page 58); from the exotic, such as the Goat Cheese Salad (page 63) to the familiar, like the spinach combinations on pages 68–69, salads are colorful and fresh-tasting overtures or accompaniments to any meal.

For the busy cook, easy make-ahead salads offer a head start on entertaining. For casual warm-weather dining, try something different, with accompaniments like savory Peas and Bacon Salad (page 66) or Radish-Sesame Salad (page 70), a tangy dish with an oriental flair. Traditional picnic fare is given a new twist in variations on the potato salad theme: Provençal (page 68) and Dilled (page 67). The Crunchy Sweet Potato Salad (page 68) is perfect for a down-home fried chicken picnic.

Pasta and grain salads, ideal as dinner party appetizers and buffet dishes, provide an appealing change of pace from the usual relish tray. Dishes such as Tabbouleh (page 76) and Garlicky Pasta Salad (page 74) can be prepared well ahead of time, and the Lasagne Spinach Rolls on page 75, topped with a creamy Gorgonzola dressing just before serving, can be readied up to two hours in advance.

Of course, no salad would be complete without a dressing. And the many flavored oils and vinegars available in supermarkets and specialty food shops have helped inspire the tempting new dressing recipes presented here. They turn even the simplest salad into a special-occasion dish. And, made months ahead of time, they are ready at a moment's notice to give an extraordinary lift to everyday fare. Some dressings, including Avocado Dressing (page 80), or Artichoke and Fresh Spinach Dressing (page 81), are thick and zesty enough to be used as dips for raw-vegetable crudités. Or try the Roquefort (page 80) or Sesame Seed (page 77) dressings as unusual sauces for lightly steamed fresh vegetables.

Mix and match the salad recipes that follow with your favorite main courses and desserts. You'll find almost unlimited possibilities for menu planning that add flair and freshness any season of the year.

❦ Vegetable Salads

Artichoke and Watercress Salad

2 servings

1 bunch watercress, thoroughly washed and dried

1 6-ounce jar marinated artichoke hearts, drained (marinade reserved)

2 tablespoons capers, rinsed and drained

Divide watercress between 2 salad plates. Top each with half the artichoke hearts and sprinkle with capers. Dress with some of reserved marinade.

Soufflé-Stuffed Artichokes

Dip the leaves into the soufflé before biting into them and then finish the last of the soufflé with the artichoke heart. Serve with a platter of thinly sliced cold meats, some crusty bread and an assortment of cheeses. Offer fresh berries splashed with liqueur for dessert.

4 to 6 servings

4 large artichokes or 6 medium artichokes, cooked

1 cup milk

2 tablespoons (¼ stick) butter

2 tablespoons all purpose flour

3 eggs, separated

¼ cup grated Gruyère cheese
Salt and freshly ground pepper
Pinch of cayenne pepper
Pinch of freshly grated nutmeg

Pinch of cream of tartar

Generously oil large baking dish. Gently spread artichoke leaves and remove chokes (thistle portion) from center with spoon. Place artichokes in dish.

Heat milk just until warm. Melt butter in small saucepan. Stir in flour and cook, without browning, 2 to 3 minutes. Remove from heat and stir in warm milk. Return to heat and bring to full boil, stirring constantly. Reduce heat and simmer 2 minutes. Remove from heat and beat in egg yolks one at a time. Add cheese and blend well. Season to taste with salt, pepper, cayenne and nutmeg. Allow to cool.

Preheat oven to 350°F. Beat egg whites until foamy. Add pinch of salt and cream of tartar and continue beating until stiff peaks form. Stir ¼ of whites into sauce to loosen. Fold in remaining whites. Fill artichokes with soufflé and bake until filling is golden brown and slightly puffed, about 20 minutes.

Green Bean, Walnut and Feta Salad

6 servings

1½ pounnds fresh green beans (ends trimmed), cut in half crosswise

¾ cup olive oil

½ cup packed fresh mint leaves, finely chopped

¼ cup white wine vinegar

¾ teaspoon salt

½ teaspoon minced garlic

¼ teaspoon freshly ground pepper

1 cup chopped toasted walnuts

1 cup diced red onion

1 cup crumbled feta cheese or coarsely grated imported Parmesan cheese

Bring 4 quarts salted water to boil in 6-quart saucepan over medium-high heat. Add beans and cook until crisp-tender, about 4 minutes. Drain well; immediately plunge into ice water to stop cooking process. Drain beans again; pat dry with paper towels. *(Can be prepared several hours ahead.)*

Combine oil, mint, vinegar, salt, garlic and pepper in processor and blend.

Arrange beans in shallow glass serving bowl. Sprinkle with nuts, onion and cheese. Just before serving, pour dressing over and toss thoroughly.

Avocado-Belgian Endive Salad

4 servings

6 ounces spinach leaves
3 heads Belgian endive
4 water chestnuts, thinly sliced
1 large firm-ripe avocado, peeled, pitted and thinly sliced into rings
4 strips bacon, cooked crisp and crumbled

Dressing
¾ cup light olive oil

¼ cup Sherry vinegar
2 tablespoons Moutarde de meaux (coarsely ground French mustard)
1 shallot, minced
¼ teaspoon dried basil or ¾ teaspoon minced fresh
Salt and freshly ground pepper

Place bed of spinach leaves on each of 4 salad plates. Separate endive leaves and arrange over spinach in flower pattern. Scatter each salad with water chestnuts and then overlapping slices of avocado. Sprinkle evenly with bacon.

Whisk dressing ingredients together until smooth. Spoon over each salad and serve immediately.

Bean Curd and Straw Mushroom Salad

2 servings

2 cups fresh or canned bean curd (tofu),* drained and cut into 1-inch cubes
1 cup drained canned straw mushrooms*
½ cup chicken broth

Spicy Peanut Dressing
3 tablespoons vegetable oil
2 tablespoons light soy sauce
½ cup finely chopped onion
1 cup water

¼ cup cream-style peanut butter
2 tablespoons vinegar
½ teaspoon dried red pepper flakes or 1 to 2 fresh jalapeño peppers, seeded and chopped
Salt

1 pound fresh spinach, stems removed
Boiling water
Juice of 1 lemon

Combine bean curd and mushrooms in heavy skillet. Add broth and simmer gently, uncovered, for 5 minutes. Remove with slotted spoon and drain well. Set on serving platter and let cool.

For dressing: Heat oil and soy sauce in small saucepan over medium heat. Add onion and cook until limp. Reduce heat to low, add next 5 ingredients and stir until smooth. Remove from heat and cool.

Place spinach in colander and pour boiling water over to wilt. Drain well and pat dry. Squeeze lemon juice over top and let stand until cool.

Ring bean curd and mushrooms with spinach. Spoon some of dressing over bean curd and mushrooms. Serve immediately with remaining dressing.

* Available in oriental markets.

Marinated Hot Carrot Salad

8 to 10 servings

5 to 6 large carrots, thinly sliced
1 4-ounce can whole jalapeño peppers, washed, seeded and deveined

1 large onion, thinly sliced
½ cup oil
½ cup white vinegar
1 teaspoon salt

Combine carrot in medium bowl with enough hot water to cover; let stand 30 minutes. Drain well. Cover with cold water. Add several ice cubes to bowl and let stand 15 minutes. Meanwhile, mix remaining ingredients in large bowl. Drain carrot. Add to pepper mixture and toss well. Cover and seal tightly. Store in refrigerator until ready to use.

Carrot and Parsnip Salad

8 servings

1 pound carrots, peeled
1 pound parsnips, peeled

2 green onions, finely chopped
3 tablespoons fresh lemon juice

¼ teaspoon *each* dry mustard, salt and freshly ground pepper
⅓ cup olive oil

Chopped fresh parsley (garnish)

Bring salted water to boil in 2 large saucepans over medium-high heat. Cook carrots and parsnips separately until tender, about 30 to 35 minutes. Drain well. Slice vegetables diagonally. Transfer to medium bowl. Keep warm.

Combine green onion, lemon juice, mustard, salt and pepper in medium bowl. Add olive oil in slow, steady stream, whisking until well blended. Pour over warm vegetables and toss.

Spoon vegetables into center of platter. Garnish with chopped fresh parsley and serve immediately.

Broccoli Salad with Chive and Tarragon Dressing

8 servings

2 to 3 bunches broccoli, trimmed and cut into medium florets with 1-inch stems

½ cup oil
2 tablespoons chopped sweet pickle
2 tablespoons chopped fresh parsley
2 tablespoons chopped red or green bell pepper

2 tablespoons tarragon vinegar
1 tablespoon chopped fresh chives
¾ teaspoon salt
¾ teaspoon sugar
Dash of garlic juice
Pinch of ground red pepper

Chopped hard-cooked egg (garnish)
Chopped pimiento (garnish)

Bring salted water to boil in large saucepan over medium-high heat. Add broccoli and cook until al dente, about 12 minutes. Immediately transfer to bowl of ice water to stop cooking process. Drain well; refrigerate.

Combine all remaining ingredients except egg and pimiento in jar with tight-fitting lid and shake well. Refrigerate.

To serve, arrange broccoli on flat platter. Pour dressing over. Garnish with chopped egg and pimiento.

Beet and Onion Salad

4 servings

4 medium-size fresh beets
4 medium-size yellow onions

1 head romaine lettuce, separated into leaves
4 hard-cooked eggs, sliced

16 cherry tomatoes
4 to 5 tablespoons Spanish Sherry wine vinegar or Italian balsamico vinegar
Freshly ground pepper

Bring 6 cups water to boil in large saucepan over medium-high heat. Add beets and cook until tender and easily pierced with knife. Drain well. Let cool. Repeat for onions. Trim off stem and root ends of beets and remove peel. Slice beets thinly. Trim off stem, root ends and first layer of onion peel. Halve each vertically.

Arrange romaine leaves on 4 salad plates. Overlap slices of beet on upper third of each plate; overlap sliced egg below beets. Place 2 onion halves cut side up in center of each plate and 4 cherry tomatoes on bottom third. Sprinkle with vinegar and pepper. Serve at room temperature.

Red Cabbage

6 servings

½ medium head red cabbage, thinly sliced
¼ cup cider vinegar
Sea salt

2 tablespoons grape-seed or safflower oil

Toss cabbage gently with vinegar and salt. Add oil and toss again.

Ranch Slaw

2 servings

1 carrot
1 zucchini
½ green pepper
1 celery stalk
¼ head white cabbage
¼ head red cabbage

2 tablespoons fresh lemon juice
1 egg yolk
1 teaspoon Dijon mustard
Salt and freshly ground pepper
Minced fresh parsley (garnish)

Dressing
⅓ cup olive oil

Cut all vegetables into fine julienne, or grate. Wrap white and red cabbage in towel and refrigerate 1 hour.

Combine vegetables in large bowl and toss lightly. Whisk all remaining ingredients except parsley in small bowl until well blended. Pour over vegetables and toss thoroughly. Sprinkle with minced parsley before serving.

Spiced Red Cabbage

6 to 8 servings

1 small head red cabbage
⅔ cup water
4 tablespoons (½ stick) butter
3 cloves
1 teaspoon salt

2 tart apples, peeled, cored and sliced
2 tablespoons sugar
2 tablespoons fresh lemon juice

Discard outer leaves of cabbage. Halve, core and rinse remainder. Shred very finely. Combine water and 2 tablespoons butter in medium skillet over medium heat. Add cabbage, cloves and salt and stir through. Add apple slices and stir to blend. Cover tightly, reduce heat to low and simmer until cabbage is tender, about 45 minutes, stirring occasionally. Add remaining butter, sugar and lemon juice and continue simmering, covered, for 5 minutes. Let cool. Cover and refrigerate overnight. Serve hot.

Swiss-Style Céleri Salad

A special first course, or serve as an accompaniment to cold sliced meats, cold baked ham or poached fish.

4 to 6 servings

1 cup mayonnaise
2 tablespoons whipping cream
1 heaping tablespoon Bavarian mustard
1 tablespoon Mustard Seed Vinegar (see recipe, page 81)
1 teaspoon salt
3 to 4 large celery roots (celeriac), peeled and coarsely grated

1 tart large green apple, coarsely grated
½ cup coarsely chopped hazelnuts, toasted
1 bunch watercress (garnish) Additional chopped hazelnuts, toasted (optional)

Mix mayonnaise, cream, mustard, vinegar and salt in mixing bowl. Add celery root and apple and toss well. Stir in hazelnuts. Cover and chill 2 hours to blend flavors. Serve heaped onto bed of watercress and garnish with additional toasted hazelnuts, if desired.

Alsatian Chicory Salad

4 servings

1 French bread baguette, sliced into rounds ⅛ inch thick
1 large garlic clove, split
1 large head curly endive
¾ pound thick-sliced bacon, cut into lardoons (½-inch sticks)
4 shallots, minced

¼ cup Garlic Oil (see recipe, page 82)
4 teaspoons Caraway Seed Vinegar (see recipe, page 84)
½ teaspoon sugar
½ teaspoon salt
Freshly ground pepper
1 to 2 tablespoons white wine

Preheat oven to 200°F. Rub bread on both sides with garlic. Place on baking sheet and toast until dry, crisp and golden brown. Set aside.

Coarsely break endive into large wooden salad bowl; set aside.

Heat skillet over medium-high heat. Add bacon and sauté until limp and pale golden. Add shallot and sauté about 1 or 2 minutes longer.

At table, pour warm bacon-shallot mixture over greens. Sprinkle with oil, vinegar, sugar, salt, pepper and wine and toss gently. Add croutons and toss.

Goat Cheese Salad

8 servings

1 pound Boston lettuce, washed, drained and crisped
¾ cup julienne of beet, well drained (optional)

4 ounces Montrachet chèvre cheese, cut into 8 slices
¼ cup toasted fine breadcrumbs

3 tablespoons unsalted butter
½ cup Basic Vinaigrette (see following recipe)
½ cup parsley leaves, minced (garnish)

Line salad bowl with lettuce leaves. Tear remaining leaves into bite-size pieces and add to bowl. Arrange beet over greens, if desired. Cover and refrigerate.

Coat cheese slices with crumbs. Wrap in plastic, pressing crumbs gently but firmly into cheese. Place in freezer.

At serving time, melt butter in large skillet over medium heat. Brown cheese on each side just until heated through. Transfer to plate. Pour vinaigrette over salad. Garnish with parsley and center with cheese slices. Serve immediately.

Basic Vinaigrette

Makes 1 cup

¾ cup oil (preferably 3 tablespoons French olive oil mixed with safflower oil)
¼ cup red wine vinegar

1 teaspoon Dijon mustard
¾ teaspoon salt
Freshly ground pepper

Mix all ingredients. Taste and adjust seasoning.

Chinese Eggplant and Pepper Salad

The smoky chipotle chilies add a delicate, unusual flavor to this traditional dish. At its best served at room temperature as an accompaniment to grilled seafoods and poultry.

4 to 6 servings

1 pound eggplant (preferably Japanese), cut into ¼ × 3-inch sticks
1 tablespoon salt

2 dried chipotle chilies, rinsed
8 large garlic cloves
6 thin slices fresh ginger
6 tablespoons vegetable oil
1 tablespoon black bean sauce

2 sweet red bell peppers, seeded and cut into thin strips

¼ teaspoon sugar
Salt and freshly ground pepper
3 tablespoons Chinese white rice vinegar
Lettuce leaves (optional garnish)

Place eggplant in colander and sprinkle with salt; drain 30 minutes.

Meanwhile, add chilies to large heavy skillet and roast over medium heat until slightly softened, about 4 minutes, watching carefully to prevent burning. Remove chilies from heat, stem and seed. Transfer to processor or blender. Add garlic, ginger, 2 tablespoons oil and bean sauce and puree.

Heat 1 tablespoon oil in wok or large skillet over high heat. Add red pepper strips and stir-fry 30 seconds. Add puree and stir-fry 40 seconds. Transfer mixture to bowl and set aside.

Rinse eggplant and drain well; pat dry with paper towels. Heat remaining 3 tablespoons oil in wok over high heat. Add eggplant and stir-fry until wilted, about 5 minutes. Blend in pepper mixture and sugar and stir-fry 30 seconds to 1 minute. Transfer to serving platter and let cool to room temperature. Season with salt and pepper to taste and sprinkle with vinegar. Garnish with lettuce leaves.

Eggplant-Pepper Salad with Pesto Dressing

Salad can be prepared 2 days ahead.

4 servings

Pesto Dressing
  1 large garlic clove
  ½ cup firmly packed fresh basil leaves
  ⅓ to ½ cup light olive oil
  ¼ cup freshly grated Parmesan cheese (preferably imported)
  2 to 3 tablespoons cider vinegar
  Salt and freshly ground pepper

Eggplant Salad
  2 medium eggplants, cut into ¼ × 3-inch pieces
  Salt

Vegetable oil
  8 ounces Italian Fontina cheese, shredded
  5 small green onions, cut julienne
  1 large green pepper, cored, seeded and cut julienne
  1 cup pickled sweet red pepper, drained and cut julienne
  ¼ cup chopped salted cashews
  Fresh basil leaves (garnish)

For dressing: Puree all ingredients in processor or blender. Transfer to jar. Cover and refrigerate up to 7 days.

For salad: Sprinkle eggplant with salt in large bowl and mix well. Transfer to colander; let drain about 30 minutes.

Position rack as close to heat source as possible and preheat broiler. Generously oil large baking sheet.

Rinse eggplant under cold water and thoroughly pat dry with paper towels. Arrange half of eggplant in single layer on prepared sheet. Sprinkle lightly with oil and broil until lightly browned, about 3 minutes. Turn slices over and broil another 3 minutes. Transfer eggplant to container with tight-fitting lid. Repeat with remaining eggplant.

Add cheese, onion, peppers and cashews to eggplant and mix well. *(Can be prepared ahead to this point. Cover and refrigerate 1 to 2 days.)* Pour dressing over eggplant mixture and toss gently. Cover and refrigerate overnight. Garnish with basil leaves before serving.

Corn Salad

4 servings

  1 7-ounce can whole kernel corn, drained
  1 4-ounce jar sliced pimientos, drained
  ¼ cup minced fresh parsley
  1 small bunch green onions, chopped
  1 green pepper, seeded and chopped
  1 red bell pepper, seeded and chopped
  10 cherry tomatoes
  Vinaigrette (see following recipe)

Combine all ingredients in glass bowl and toss thoroughly. Serve chilled.

Vinaigrette

Makes about ½ cup

  7 tablespoons olive oil
  2 tablespoons white wine vinegar
  ¼ teaspoon dried tarragon
  ¼ teaspoon dry mustard
  ¼ teaspoon salt
  Freshly ground pepper

Combine all ingredients in bowl or jar with tight-fitting lid, and whisk or shake until thoroughly blended.

Fennel Salad with Gorgonzola Dressing

2 servings

1 fennel bulb, trimmed and cut into thin slices
4 mushrooms, thinly sliced
2 radishes, thinly sliced
2 tablespoons minced fresh chives
2 tablespoons minced fresh parsley
1 tablespoon minced red onion
2 tablespoons olive oil

1½ teaspoons fresh lemon juice
½ teaspoon Dijon mustard
Salt and freshly ground pepper
2 tablespoons crumbled Gorgonzola cheese
Lettuce leaves
Olives and lemon wedges (garnish)

Combine first 6 ingredients in medium bowl. Whisk oil, lemon juice and mustard in small bowl. Season with salt and pepper. Stir in cheese. Pour over salad and toss well. Arrange lettuce leaves on individual plates and mound salad in center. Garnish each serving with olives and lemon wedges.

Romaine Salad with Cashews

12 servings

Dressing
¼ cup cider vinegar
1 generous tablespoon Dijon mustard
Salt and freshly ground pepper
Pinch of ground cumin
Pinch of ground cardamom
½ to ¾ cup light olive oil

Salad
3 heads romaine lettuce, rinsed, dried and broken into bite-size pieces
1 cup salted cashews
½ cup thinly sliced sweet red onion
½ cup garbanzo beans (chick-peas), rinsed and drained

For dressing: Combine all ingredients and blend well. Adjust seasoning.
For salad: Combine all ingredients.
Just before serving, stir dressing again. Add to salad and toss lightly.

Caesar Salad

6 servings

Dressing
½ cup oil
6 anchovy fillets, drained and finely chopped
1 garlic clove, minced
1½ teaspoons Worcestershire sauce
½ teaspoon salt
½ teaspoon dry mustard
¼ teaspoon freshly ground pepper

Salad
1 egg
½ garlic clove
2 large bunches romaine lettuce
¼ cup fresh lemon juice
1 cup seasoned croutons
¼ cup grated Parmesan cheese

For dressing: Combine all ingredients in jar with tight-fitting lid and shake well. Refrigerate.

For salad: Pour water into small saucepan to depth of 2 inches. Bring to boil over medium-high heat. Turn off heat. Place egg in pan and let stand 1 minute. Remove with slotted spoon.

Rub inside of salad bowl with garlic. Tear lettuce into bowl. Add dressing and toss lightly. Break egg over lettuce. Pour lemon juice over egg and toss again. Sprinkle croutons and cheese over top and toss well. Serve immediately.

Onion Panade

A mellow variation of the Provençal dish traditionally made with bread. Can be prepared several days ahead and refrigerated. Serve at room temperature.

6 appetizer servings

6 tablespoons olive oil
6 medium-large onions (about 2 pounds), thinly sliced
½ teaspoon salt
1 tablespoon anise liqueur

1 tablespoon chopped fresh sage or 1 teaspoon dried, crumbled

Niçoise olives and small toast slices

Heat olive oil in large heavy skillet over low heat. Add onion, sprinkle with salt and stir to coat with oil. Cover and cook 40 minutes, stirring occasionally. Remove cover and continue cooking just until onion begin to color, about 20 minutes. Add liqueur and sage and cook 10 more minutes. Cool to room temperature.

To serve, spoon onion mixture into center of large platter. Garnish with olives. Accompany with toast.

Endive and Walnut Salad

2 servings

2 heads Belgian endive, quartered lengthwise
¼ cup coarsely chopped walnuts
2 tablespoons walnut oil or olive oil

1 tablespoon fresh lemon juice
Salt and freshly ground pepper

Divide endive spears evenly between 2 salad plates. Sprinkle with walnuts. Whisk together oil and lemon juice. Season with salt and pepper. Drizzle dressing evenly over endive.

Chateau Salad

2 servings

½ head Bibb lettuce
½ head romaine lettuce
3 tablespoons olive oil
1 tablespoon garlic wine vinegar
¾ teaspoon dried chervil, crumbled
¾ teaspoon Beau Monde seasoning

¼ teaspoon dried sweet basil, crumbled
¼ teaspoon dried marjoram, crumbled
Salt and freshly ground pepper

Tear lettuce into large bowl. Combine remaining ingredients in a jar with tight-fitting lid and shake well. Just before serving, pour over salad and toss.

Peas and Bacon Salad

6 servings

1 cup sour cream
1 teaspoon seasoned salt
¼ teaspoon lemon pepper
¼ teaspoon garlic powder
1 20-ounce bag frozen peas, thawed (not cooked)

½ pound bacon, cooked, drained and crumbled
1 small tomato, diced
¼ cup minced red onion

Combine sour cream and seasonings in a medium bowl. Add remaining ingredients, mix thoroughly and chill for several hours or overnight.

Extra crumbled bacon may be stored in small plastic bags in freezer until ready to use.

🍎 Salad

When in doubt about the choice of a first course, or the last, or even when the selection of an entrée poses a question, consider the salad. Its ability to change forms at the whim of the cook lends diversity to any meal, as it can be fitted effortlessly into practically any slot on the menu, including dessert.

The French divide salads into two major categories: *simples,* consisting of fresh greens dressed with vinaigrette or a single cooked or uncooked vegetable, chilled and similarly dressed; and *composées,* a mixture of cooked or uncooked ingredients, often dressed elaborately. Fruit and chef's salads, aspics and other variations fall into this category.

In Europe salads are often listed among the *antipasti, Vorspeisen* or *hors d'oeuvre*—as a first course designed to whet the appetite. If you favor this approach, choose something light and piquant such as asparagus vinaigrette or an aspic. If your salad is to accompany the main course, classic tossed greens are ideal, but the composition must be carefully orchestrated to complement the entrée. A green salad, served alone or with cheese, can also provide a refreshing break after the main course. When the occasion calls for a light dessert, a salad of fruits macerated in brandy or liqueur is a good choice.

Simple does not always mean easy—special care must be taken with the plain salad, as its very simplicity invites monotony. It is important to create a contrast in texture, color and flavor; try pairing romaine or Boston lettuce with watercress or spinach, for example, with a bit of endive or escarole for added tang. Don't overdo it, however—two or three greens are adequate. Particular attention must also be paid to the dressing. A plain salad is traditionally dressed with Sauce Vinaigrette, but the choice of oil and vinegar, their proportion, and the style and degree of flavoring depend on the greens. Lettuces such as Boston, Bibb and iceberg, whose delicate flavors are easily overpowered, team best with lemon juice and the lighter oils (such as a combination of safflower and light French olive oil) and gentle seasoning—perhaps a little finely minced shallot, salt and freshly ground pepper and a fresh herb. Romaine, escarole, arugala and chicory, on the other hand, demand a more robust dressing, made with a hearty red wine vinegar and a full-flavored oil, and seasoned with mustard, pungent herbs and garlic.

Dilled Potato Salad

12 servings

3 egg yolks, room temperature
1 tablespoon Dijon mustard
1 tablespoon wine vinegar or cider vinegar
1 cup light olive oil
½ cup vegetable oil
Salt and freshly ground pepper

⅔ cup minced fresh dill
6 pounds new potatoes, boiled, peeled and diced
⅔ cup finely chopped sweet red onion
Fresh dill sprigs (optional garnish)

Combine yolks, mustard and vinegar in processor or blender and mix until thick and smooth, about 2 minutes. With machine running, gradually add oils through feed tube in slow, steady stream, stopping machine occasionally to be sure oil is being absorbed (add 2 tablespoons very hot water if mixture begins to separate), until mayonnaise is very thick. Season with salt and pepper.

Transfer to large container and blend in dill. Gently fold in potato and onion, coating well. Refrigerate overnight. Garnish with fresh dill sprigs.

Provençal Potato Salad

6 servings

7 tablespoons minced green onion
3 tablespoons red wine vinegar
1½ tablespoons minced anchovy fillet (about 3)
½ teaspoon sugar
½ cup virgin olive oil
¼ cup Pistou (see recipe, page 30)
5 to 5½ pounds new potatoes (about 10 large), cooked until tender, peeled and cut into ½-inch-thick slices (keep warm)

24 tiny Mediterranean olives, pitted (garnish)
Thinly sliced green onion (garnish)
Coarsely cracked pepper (garnish)

Combine onion, vinegar, anchovy and sugar in large bowl and mix well. Gradually whisk in olive oil in slow, steady stream. Add pistou and whisk until blended. Add warm potato and mix very gently until all slices are coated with dressing. Let cool to room temperature. Mix gently again before serving. Garnish with olives, sliced green onion and coarsely cracked pepper.

Crunchy Sweet Potato Salad

6 servings

2 cups peeled and grated uncooked sweet potato
1¼ to 1½ cups finely chopped green pepper
1 cup finely chopped almonds or cashews

½ cup diced peeled cucumber
3 tablespoons lemon yogurt
Lettuce leaves
Cucumber slices (garnish)
Lemon yogurt

Combine sweet potato, green pepper, nuts and ½ cup cucumber in large bowl and toss lightly. Add 3 tablespoons yogurt, stirring to blend well. Arrange lettuce leaves on platter. Mound salad in center. Garnish with cucumber slices. Serve with additional lemon yogurt.

Spinach Salad

Dressing can be prepared ahead and refrigerated up to 1 week. Reheat before serving.

4 servings

Salad
1 large bunch spinach, washed and stemmed
1 large red apple, unpeeled, cored and coarsely chopped
¼ cup salted peanuts

Dressing
4 eggs, well beaten

½ to 1 cup sugar
¼ cup dry mustard
2 teaspoons salt
2 cups whipping cream
⅔ cup white vinegar

For salad: Tear spinach leaves into large bowl. Sprinkle with apple and peanuts.
For dressing: Combine eggs, ½ cup sugar, mustard and salt in medium bowl and mix well. Slowly stir in 1 cup cream with vinegar. Transfer to heavy saucepan and cook slowly over medium heat until thickened. Remove from heat. Whisk in remaining cream. Taste and add remaining sugar as desired. Pour dressing over spinach mixture, toss thoroughly and serve.

Roasted Pepper and Dandelion Salad

Peppers can be roasted several days ahead and refrigerated. Bring to room temperature before combining with other ingredients.

6 to 8 servings

4 large red bell peppers

5 cups young dandelion greens, arugula or escarole

½ small red onion, thinly sliced

6 tablespoons olive oil

3 to 4 tablespoons wine vinegar
Salt and freshly ground pepper

Roast peppers on grill over hot fire until charred on all sides. Transfer to paper bag, close tightly and let stand about 1 hour. Peel off skin. Discard stem and seeds. Slice peppers into thin strips.

When ready to serve, combine remaining ingredients in salad bowl and toss lightly. Add pepper strips and toss again.

The Magnolia Hotel's Spinach Salad

8 servings

Dressing

1 medium onion, grated

1 cup oil

⅔ cup sugar

⅓ cup catsup

¼ cup red wine vinegar

Salad

1 large bunch fresh spinach, washed thoroughly, patted dry and torn into bite-size pieces

1 8-ounce can water chestnuts, drained and chopped

1 cup fresh bean sprouts

¼ cup (or more) chopped cooked bacon

2 hard-cooked eggs, grated

For dressing: Combine ingredients in jar with tight-fitting lid and shake well.

For salad: Combine spinach, water chestnuts, bean sprouts and ¼ cup bacon in large salad bowl and toss gently. Add dressing to taste and toss again. Sprinkle with grated egg (and additional bacon, if desired) and serve.

Ma Maison's Spinach Salad

6 servings

Mustard-Vinaigrette Dressing

2 tablespoons Sherry wine vinegar

2 egg yolks

2 teaspoons Dijon mustard

2 teaspoons chopped fresh tarragon

¼ teaspoon salt
Pinch of freshly ground pepper

2 cups oil

2 pounds spinach, stems discarded, leaves washed and dried

3 cups shredded Swiss cheese

¾ pound mushrooms, sliced

½ pound bacon, crisply cooked, drained and chopped

3 hard-cooked eggs, chopped
Tomato wedges (garnish)

Combine first 6 ingredients in medium bowl and blend well with whisk. Slowly add oil in steady stream, whisking constantly. Store in tightly covered container. *(Can be refrigerated up to 1 week.)*

Place spinach in large salad bowl. Add cheese, mushrooms, bacon and egg and toss with just enough dressing to coat lightly. Arrange on chilled individual plates and garnish with tomato. Serve with additional dressing.

Radish-Sesame Salad

2 servings

1 large bunch red radishes, trimmed and thinly sliced into rounds
1 tablespoon white vinegar
1½ teaspoons sugar or to taste
1 teaspoon Japanese soy sauce

2 dashes sesame oil
2 teaspoons toasted sesame seed
Radish leaves (optional garnish)

Combine radish, vinegar, sugar, soy sauce and sesame oil in container with tight-fitting lid and shake well. Cover and refrigerate overnight.

To serve, sprinkle mixture with sesame seed and garnish with radish leaves, if desired.

Squash and Pecan Sauté in Zucchini Shells

Can be prepared several hours ahead, covered and kept at room temperature. Reheat in 300°F oven for 10 minutes.

4 servings

2 large zucchini (1 pound each), halved lengthwise
Salt
3 to 4 small zucchini (about 1¾ pounds total)
3 to 4 small yellow crookneck squash (about 1¾ pounds total)
2½ tablespoons salt

1 tablespoon unsalted butter
⅔ cup coarsely chopped pecans

1 tablespoon unsalted butter, room temperature

2 tablespoons (¼ stick) unsalted butter
1 to 2 tablespoons fresh lemon juice
3 4-inch sprigs fresh thyme (leaves only)
Salt and freshly ground white pepper

4 tablespoons finely chopped pecans
Pecan halves (garnish)

Scoop pulp from large zucchini, leaving ¼-inch shell (if pulp is not too seedy, reserve for another use). Sprinkle inside of zucchini shells generously with salt. Invert on wire rack set in pan. Drain 1 hour. Meanwhile, grate small zucchini and crookneck squash. Alternate layers of grated squash and 2½ tablespoons salt in colander, ending with salt. Cover completely with plate. Weight with heavy object. Let stand in pan or sink about 1 hour to drain.

Melt 1 tablespoon butter in small skillet over medium heat. Stir in ⅔ cup coarsely chopped pecans and cook, stirring frequently, until golden, about 3 to 4 minutes. Set aside.

Preheat oven to 350°F. Rinse zucchini shells in cold water to remove salt; pat dry. Spread shells inside and out with 1 tablespoon butter. Invert on baking sheet. Bake zucchini shells just until tender, about 30 minutes.

Rinse grated squash thoroughly in cold water to remove salt; squeeze dry in potato ricer or towel. Melt 2 tablespoons butter in wok or large skillet over high heat. Add grated squash, lemon juice and thyme and stir-fry until all moisture has evaporated, about 2 to 3 minutes. Stir in coarsely chopped pecans. Season with salt and pepper.

Sprinkle inside of each zucchini shell with 1 tablespoon finely chopped pecans. Fill with stir-fried squash. Garnish with pecan halves and serve.

Tomato Salad with Lentils

4 servings

½ pound (about 1 cup) red or
   yellow lentils, sorted

4 cups water
1 onion pierced with 4 cloves
1 carrot, quartered
1 parsley sprig
1 3-inch thyme sprig
1 bay leaf
   Salt and freshly ground pepper

6 anchovies

1 garlic clove
2 tablespoons red wine vinegar
6 tablespoons olive oil
3 cornichons, minced
1 tablespoon minced fresh chervil
   Salt and freshly ground pepper

2 ounces green beans, trimmed

4 large beefsteak tomatoes
2 tablespoons minced fresh chives
   (garnish)

Combine lentils in heavy large saucepan with enough cold water to cover. Let stand for 24 hours.

Drain lentils; rinse and drain again. Return to saucepan. Add 4 cups water, onion, carrot, parsley, thyme and bay leaf. Bring to simmer, then cover tightly and cook over lowest possible heat, stirring occasionally, until lentils are tender but still retain shape, about 45 to 50 minutes. Drain well. Transfer to large bowl. Discard onion, carrot and herbs. Season with salt and pepper.

Combine anchovies and garlic in mortar or wooden bowl and pound to paste. Transfer to small bowl. Whisk in vinegar, then add olive oil in slow, steady stream. Stir in minced cornichons and chervil. Season with salt and pepper. Add to lentils and toss gently. Marinate at least 2 hours.

Bring large pot of salted water to rapid boil over high heat. Add green beans and cook until crisp-tender, about 3 minutes. Drain beans and plunge into ice water to stop cooking process. Drain well; pat dry. Cut beans diagonally into long, narrow slivers.

Core tomatoes carefully. Cut each into 8 wedges without cutting completely through to bottom. Gently open into flower shape. Place tomatoes on individual plates. Taste lentil mixture and adjust seasoning. Spoon evenly into tomatoes. Arrange green bean slivers attractively between wedges. Sprinkle with chives. Serve at room temperature.

Green Salad with Sweet and Sour Dressing

The dressing from this recipe can also be used as a dip.

4 to 6 servings

3 hard-cooked eggs, separated
⅓ cup oil
¼ cup sugar
½ teaspoon salt
½ teaspoon celery seed

⅓ cup vinegar
   Freshly ground pepper
   Assorted salad greens torn into
   bite-size pieces

Mash egg yolks in small bowl; chop whites separately and refrigerate. Blend oil, sugar, salt and celery seed with yolks. Cover and chill. Just before serving, add vinegar and pepper and mix thoroughly. Pour over salad greens and toss lightly. Sprinkle with chopped egg white.

Vegetable Vinaigrette Salad

4 to 6 servings

1 head cauliflower, separated into florets
1 pound green beans, trimmed, ends removed
1 pound small mushrooms
2 medium zucchini, cut into chunks
    Vinaigrette Dressing (see following recipe)

1 15-ounce can plum tomatoes, drained
¼ cup (or more) capers, drained
1 2-ounce tin anchovies, patted dry
1 bunch green onions, sliced

Separately steam cauliflower, green beans, mushrooms and zucchini until crisp-tender. Drain vegetables if necessary and place in medium bowl. Pour vinaigrette over, cover and refrigerate overnight.

One hour before serving, add tomatoes, capers, anchovies and green onion. Cover and refrigerate. Toss lightly just before serving.

Vinaigrette Dressing

Makes about 3½ cups

2 cups vegetable oil
1 cup garlic vinegar
5 tablespoons Dijon mustard
    Juice of 1 lemon

1 teaspoon garlic salt
1 teaspoon cumin
    Salt and freshly ground pepper

In medium bowl or jar with lid, thoroughly mix all ingredients.

Moroccan Vegetable Salad

This is nice with lavosh, *the Greek cracker bread, or with whole wheat crackers.*

4 to 5 servings

½ pound small whole mushrooms
1½ cups cooked garbanzo beans
1 cup pitted large black olives
¾ cup coarsely chopped green onion
2 green bell peppers, chopped
2 red bell peppers, chopped
1 dozen cherry tomatoes

1 cup yogurt

½ cup mayonnaise
2 garlic cloves, mashed
2 tablespoons olive oil
1 tablespoon lemon juice
1 teaspoon powdered cumin
⅛ teaspoon turmeric
    Salt and freshly ground pepper
    Lettuce leaves

Steam mushrooms 5 minutes; cool. Combine with beans, olives, green onion, peppers and tomatoes and chill 2 hours.

Mix yogurt, mayonnaise, garlic, olive oil, lemon juice, cumin, turmeric, salt and pepper and chill 2 hours. Just before serving, lightly coat mushroom mixture with dressing. Serve on lettuce leaves. Pass remaining dressing.

Smesena Salata (Hearty Vegetable Salad)

8 to 10 servings

¾ cup olive oil
¾ cup vegetable oil
½ cup red wine vinegar
⅓ cup chopped fresh parsley
2 tablespoons fresh lemon juice
1 garlic clove, minced
2 teaspoons dried basil, crumbled
¾ teaspoon salt
¼ teaspoon freshly ground pepper

3 large boiling potatoes, peeled, cooked and thinly sliced
1½ pounds baby carrots, cooked
1½ pounds green beans, cooked and cut same length as carrots
3 beets, cooked and thinly sliced

Lettuce leaves

Mix together oils, vinegar, parsley, lemon juice, garlic, basil, salt and pepper. Place potato, carrot and beans in 1 bowl and beet in smaller bowl. Pour vinaigrette over vegetables and stir gently. Cover and marinate 3 hours at room temperature or refrigerate overnight.

To serve, line platter with lettuce leaves. Arrange vegetables over top.

Mozzarella, Tomato and Fresh Basil Pesto Salad

4 servings

4 large ripe beefsteak tomatoes, each cut into 4 to 6 slices
8 ounces fresh mozzarella cheese (preferably buffalo milk mozzarella), Italian Fontina or Bel Paese, cut into same number of slices as tomatoes

½ cup Fresh Basil Pesto, room temperature (see following recipe)
¼ to ½ cup virgin olive oil
Salt and freshly ground pepper

Divide tomato and cheese into 4 equal portions. Arrange 1 slice of cheese over each tomato slice. Spread thin layer of pesto over cheese. Continue layering in same order for each portion, ending with pesto. Arrange salad in circle on platter, overlapping portions slightly. Serve at room temperature. Pass olive oil, salt and pepper separately.

Fresh Basil Pesto

Make large quantities while fresh basil leaves are at their prime and freeze pesto to be enjoyed year round.

Makes 1⅔ cups

2 cups packed fresh basil leaves
2 large garlic cloves
½ cup pine nuts

¾ cup freshly grated Parmesan or Romano cheese
⅔ cup olive oil

With mortar and pestle: Mince basil leaves finely. Transfer to mortar and crush to fine paste. Add garlic and work into paste. Gradually add pine nuts and crush until smooth. Blend in cheese. Add olive oil to mixture in slow, steady stream, stirring constantly.

With processor: Combine basil and garlic in work bowl and blend to fine paste, scraping down sides of bowl as necessary. Add pine nuts and cheese and process until smooth. With machine running, pour olive oil through feed tube in slow, steady stream and mix until smooth and creamy; if pesto is too thick, gradually pour up to ¼ cup warm water through feed tube with machine running.

Transfer pesto to jar. Cover surface of pesto with film of olive oil about ⅛ inch thick. Seal jar with tight-fitting lid. Refrigerate up to 3 months or freeze. Stir oil into pesto before using.

🍏 Pasta and Grain Salads

Spaghetti Salad

24 servings

2 pounds spaghetti
2 tablespoons olive oil
3 pounds mozzarella cheese, shredded
12 tomatoes, chopped
6 bunches watercress, finely chopped
4 garlic cloves, finely minced
3 pounds fresh pea pods

3 10-ounce packages frozen green peas, thawed
Salt and freshly ground pepper
Freshly grated Parmesan cheese

Cook spaghetti in large pot of boiling water with olive oil until al dente. Drain well. Return to pot, add mozzarella and toss until cheese melts (cheese will be gummy and seemingly inseparable but will break up as other ingredients are added). Cook over low heat 15 minutes. Remove from heat, add remaining ingredients except Parmesan and toss gently but thoroughly, using hands if necessary. Serve at room temperature. Pass bowl of Parmesan cheese separately.

Garlicky Pasta Salad

6 to 8 servings

1 pound rotini pasta, cooked al dente and drained
1 cup chopped onion
1 cup finely chopped green onion
1 cup sliced black olives
1 cup chopped green pepper
1 cup chopped tomato
1 cup chopped celery
1 cup fresh broccoli florets
1 cup chopped watercress
1 6- to 8-ounce bottle Italian salad dressing

½ to 1 teaspoon garlic powder
Salt and freshly ground pepper
1 to 2 hard-cooked eggs, chopped (optional garnish)
Anchovy fillets (optional garnish)

Combine first 9 ingredients in large bowl and toss lightly. Add dressing and seasoning and toss again. Cover and refrigerate at least 6 hours. Garnish with egg and anchovies before serving, if desired.

Lasagne Spinach Rolls with Gorgonzola Dressing

6 servings

Gorgonzola Dressing
6 ounces Gorgonzola cheese, finely crumbled
4 to 6 tablespoons fresh lemon juice
2 tablespoons Dijon mustard
2 cups whipping cream
Salt

Spinach Filling
2 pounds fresh spinach, stems removed

¼ pound prosciutto, finely chopped
4 hard-cooked eggs, chopped
¼ cup finely chopped sweet red onion
1 garlic clove, minced

8 lasagne noodles

Shredded escarole leaves (garnish)
⅓ cup toasted pine nuts (garnish)

For dressing: Combine cheese with lemon juice and mustard in medium bowl and mix well; do not mash to paste. Gradually stir in cream. Season with salt to taste. Refrigerate.

For filling: Wash spinach thoroughly (do not dry). Transfer to large saucepan. Cover and cook over medium-high heat, stirring occasionally, until wilted, about 5 minutes. Cool and squeeze dry (you should have about 2 cups cooked spinach). Chop spinach finely; *do not use processor.* Transfer to large bowl. Add prosciutto, egg, onion and garlic. Season with salt to taste and toss lightly. Stir in ½ cup plus 2 tablespoons Gorgonzola dressing.

Bring large amount of salted water to rapid boil. Stir in lasagne noodles and cook until just tender but firm to the bite (al dente), 10 to 12 minutes. Drain and rinse under cold water. Drain and pat dry with paper towels. Arrange noodles on work surface. Spread filling evenly over noodles, leaving 1-inch border on 1 short end of each (about ½ cup filling per noodle). Starting at borderless short end, roll noodle up tightly jelly roll style. Transfer to platter seam side down. Cover and refrigerate for up to 2 hours.

To serve, arrange bed of shredded escarole on individual plates. Using sharp knife, cut each roll into 3 equal slices. Arrange 4 slices cut side up on each plate. Spoon dressing over tops. Sprinkle with pine nuts and serve.

Rice, Almond and Bacon Salad

5 to 6 main-course or 8 side-dish servings

4 cups cooked brown rice
1 cup chopped green onions
1 cup chopped red pepper
¾ cup coarsely chopped almonds
½ cup corn, cooked
½ cup peas, cooked
¼ cup finely chopped cilantro*
4 slices bacon, crisply fried and crumbled

1 cup yogurt
½ cup mayonnaise
1½ tablespoons red wine vinegar
1 garlic clove, mashed
1½ teaspoons chili powder
½ teaspoon powdered cumin
Salt and pepper
Romaine lettuce (optional)

Combine first 8 ingredients. Mix yogurt, mayonnaise, wine vinegar, garlic, chili powder and cumin. Fold dressing carefully into rice mixture and add salt and pepper to taste. Place on romaine and serve immediately, or chill if preferred.

*Also called coriander or Chinese parsley. Available at Mexican and oriental markets and some supermarket produce sections.

Vegetable Rice Salad

Perfect with cold roasted meat and chicken, this salad can be made 1 day ahead and chilled. Bring to room temperature before serving.

6 servings

Vegetable Rice Salad
 2 cups cooked long-grain brown rice
 ¼ cup finely sliced radish (about 3 large)
 ½ cup peeled, seeded and finely diced cucumber
 ½ cup finely diced red bell pepper
 ¼ cup finely diced celery
 ¼ cup thinly sliced green onion
   Salt and freshly ground white pepper

Dressing
 ¼ cup olive oil
 ¼ cup freshly grated Parmesan cheese
 3 tablespoons cider vinegar
 2 tablespoons plain yogurt
 1 tablespoon minced fresh basil (or other fresh herb)
 ½ teaspoon prepared mustard
 ½ teaspoon salt
 ¼ teaspoon freshly ground pepper

   Lettuce leaves (garnish)
   Tomato wedges (garnish)
 2 tablespoons toasted pumpkin seeds (optional garnish)

For salad: Combine all ingredients in large bowl. Taste and adjust seasoning.
For dressing: Blend all ingredients in medium mixing bowl.

Add dressing to salad, mixing well. Taste and adjust seasoning. Cover tightly and refrigerate overnight.

To serve, bring salad to room temperature. Arrange lettuce leaves on large serving platter. Toss salad lightly and mound in center. Garnish with tomato wedges. Sprinkle with toasted pumpkin seeds if desired.

Tabbouleh

2 servings

 ½ cup fine bulgur
 3 cups water
 ¼ cup chopped fresh parsley
 ¼ cup chopped green onion
 3 tablespoons fresh lemon juice
 3 tablespoons olive oil
 1 tomato, peeled, seeded and chopped
 1 tablespoon chopped green pepper
 1 teaspoon grated lemon peel
   Salt and freshly ground pepper

Soak bulgur in water 30 to 60 minutes. Drain and squeeze dry. Transfer to medium bowl. Add remaining ingredients and mix well. Taste and adjust seasoning. Cover and chill before serving.

❧ Dressings

Chuck's Special Dressing

Makes about 1 cup

 ½ cup olive oil
 ¼ cup fresh lemon juice
 3 tablespoons white wine vinegar (preferably French)*
 1 egg yolk
 ¼ teaspoon dried thyme, crumbled
   Salt and freshly ground pepper

Mix oil, lemon juice, vinegar, egg yolk and thyme in small bowl. Season with salt and pepper. Cover tightly and refrigerate until ready to use.

*For a milder dressing, use only 1½ tablespoons white wine vinegar.

Stox II House Dressing

Makes about 3 cups

4 tablespoons fresh lemon juice
2 tablespoons Dijon mustard
4 teaspoons red wine vinegar
1 egg yolk
2 teaspoons whole fresh tarragon leaves or ¾ teaspoon dried, crumbled

2 teaspoons whole fresh thyme leaves or ¾ teaspoon dried, crumbled
1½ teaspoons freshly ground pepper
Salt
2 cups oil

Combine 2 tablespoons lemon juice with mustard, vinegar, egg yolk and seasoning in medium bowl of electric mixer. Beat at medium speed until thick, 2 to 3 minutes. Gradually add oil, beating constantly until mixture is smooth and creamy, about 3 minutes. Blend in remaining 2 tablespoons lemon juice. Store dressing in tightly covered container in refrigerator.

Sesame Seed Dressing

Serve this on romaine lettuce or fresh spinach leaves.

Makes 1¼ cups

½ cup sesame oil
¼ cup honey
¼ cup vinegar
3 tablespoons toasted sesame seed, ground

2 tablespoons fresh lemon juice
⅛ teaspoon garlic juice

Combine all ingredients in jar with tight-fitting lid and shake well. Refrigerate until ready to use.

Thousand Island Dressing

Makes 4 cups

1½ cups mayonnaise
1 cup whipping cream, stiffly whipped
½ cup catsup
½ cup minced celery
⅓ cup minced sweet red pepper or drained canned pimiento

⅓ cup minced fresh parsley
2 tablespoons grated onion
1 tablespoon fresh lemon juice
1 teaspoon sugar
Salt and freshly ground pepper
Cayenne pepper

Combine all ingredients in mixing bowl and blend well. Taste and adjust seasoning as necessary. Cover and chill.

❦ Sauce Vinaigrette

Sauce vinaigrette, the basic French salad dressing, is a simple combination of oil and vinegar flavored with salt and pepper and sometimes mustard and herbs. In France, it is usually made with wine vinegar, but other vinegars create different flavors, each of which has its distinctive appeal. The choice of oil also influences the flavor of the dressing. Although the traditional ratio of oil to vinegar is 3 to 1, the proportion is strictly a matter of taste, and can range from 4 to 1 to a mixture of 1 to 1. Experimentation is the only way to arrive at the perfect blend.

Basic Sauce Vinaigrette

Makes about ½ cup

1 small to medium garlic clove, peeled
1 teaspoon coarse salt
½ teaspoon freshly ground pepper (white preferred) or to taste
½ teaspoon dry mustard
1 teaspoon Dijon or Düsseldorf mustard

1 egg, beaten, or 2 tablespoons whipping cream (optional)*
2 tablespoons olive oil
2 tablespoons tarragon vinegar or wine vinegar
1 teaspoon fresh lemon juice
¼ cup vegetable oil (peanut, corn, safflower, etc.)

Cover cutting surface with a brown paper bag. Place garlic and salt on paper and mince together until they almost form a paste (brown paper absorbs some of the pungent oil, softening the strong garlic flavor). Transfer garlic and salt to mixing bowl. Add pepper, mustards, egg or cream (if desired) and olive oil. Stir vigorously with whisk or wooden spoon. Slowly add vinegar and lemon juice, stirring constantly. Continuing to stir, add vegetable oil drop by drop until all has been absorbed.

* A little egg or cream smooths dressing and keeps it from separating.

Vinegars

All vinegars have an alcohol base, the nature of which determines the character of the vinegar. Through fermentation it becomes nonalcoholic.

- *Distilled:* Fermented from grain alcohol, it has a strong, sharp aroma. Used primarily for cooking and pickling.
- *Cider:* A base of hard apple cider gives it a full-bodied aroma with a hint of fruity flavor. Taste is sharp and color is golden.
- *Malt:* Obtained through further fermenting of malt alcohol or beer. Pale to dark ginger in color, it has a distinctive flavor and light beer aroma. Popular in England with fish and chips.
- *Red Wine:* The full-bodied flavor of the wine from which it is made comes through. Flavor and color vary greatly depending on the grape variety used, the degree of dilution, processing and aging. An excellent seasoning in salad dressings and for general cooking.
- *White Wine:* Its light golden color, delicate aroma and subtle flavor make it an excellent choice for salads and cooking.
- *Herb or Seasoned:* Herbs and spices create exotic variations on either red or white wine vinegar. Garlic, tarragon, cloves, mace, allspice, basil, thyme and rosemary are all excellent flavor additives. For an unusual twist, use raspberries, chili, horseradish or mint.

Herb Vinegar

Makes 1 quart

1 tablespoon chopped fresh mint	3 bay leaves
1 tablespoon chopped fresh chives	½ cinnamon stick
1 tablespoon chopped shallot	¼ teaspoon nutmeg
1 tablespoon dried savory	1 quart mild white distilled vinegar,
1 tablespoon brown sugar	heated to boiling
1 teaspoon salt	

Combine herbs and seasonings in a large bottle or jar with tight-fitting lid. Pour vinegar over, cover and let stand 10 days, shaking once a day. Strain.

Oils

- *Olive Oil:* The spectrum ranges from French with its pale gold color and delicate flavor to the deep gold, strongly olive-flavored Spanish oils. Italian and Greek varieties fall in between. Italian is the most commonly used. No matter what its country of origin, olive oil obtained from the first pressing has the richest flavor and fullest aroma. Buy olive oil in small quantities because it can become rancid with time. If the flavor of olive oil is too strong for your taste, it can be tempered with the addition of other vegetable oils.

- *Corn:* Mild; excellent in salad dressings and for general cooking.

- *Safflower:* Similar to corn oil in flavor, but lighter in color.

- *Peanut:* Pale in color and almost flavorless, perfect when you do not want the taste of the food altered by oil. Used frequently in oriental stir-fry cooking; also good in salad dressings.

- *Sesame:* Because of its strong flavor, it must be used sparingly. Popular in oriental cooking as a seasoning.

- *Walnut:* Delicious but expensive; gives vinaigrette a wonderful nutty flavor.

- *Salads:* An all-encompassing term referring to a blend of mild-flavored oils.

Great Hints

- Prepare vinaigrette in bottom of salad bowl. Place clean, well-dried greens over dressing (only one or two leaves will touch dressing). Cover with plastic wrap and refrigerate. Salad will stay crisp and fresh for six hours or more. Toss just before serving.

- Be sure salad greens are dry or dressing will not cling to the leaves.

- If you prefer to have guests dress their own salads from separate cruets of vinegar and oil, be sure they pour vinegar over greens first, then the oil. If oil is added first it coats the greens, preventing vinegar from penetrating.

- Vinaigrette should come in contact with lettuce only at the last possible moment before serving. If it is being used to dress shredded cabbage or sliced tomatoes, it can be added up to one hour ahead of serving time.

Roquefort Dressing

Makes about 1½ cups

1 cup lowfat cottage cheese
½ cup buttermilk
2 tablespoons white wine vinegar

2 ounces Roquefort or bleu cheese
Salt and freshly ground pepper

Mix cottage cheese, buttermilk and vinegar in processor or blender. If you prefer a smooth dressing, add Roquefort or bleu cheese and mix until smooth, then season to taste with salt and pepper. If you like chunks of Roquefort, add only half of the cheese and mix until smooth. Crumble remaining cheese and stir into dressing with salt and pepper.

Herbed Dressing

Makes 3 cups

1⅓ cups white wine tarragon vinegar
1 cup safflower oil
⅔ cup olive oil
4 teaspoons mayonnaise
4 large garlic cloves, minced

2 teaspoons Dijon mustard
1 teaspoon salt
1 teaspoon brown sugar
1 teaspoon dried thyme
½ teaspoon dried tarragon

Combine all ingredients in container with tight lid and shake well. (Do not use blender; garlic should remain minced.) Pour into bottles, distributing garlic evenly. Cork or cap tightly. Keep refrigerated. Shake well before using.

Avocado Dressing

Makes about 1¼ cups

1 ripe medium avocado, peeled and pitted
½ cup Slim Crème Fraîche (see following recipe) or commercial sour half and half

1 garlic clove, chopped
2 tablespoons plain lowfat yogurt
1 tablespoon red wine vinegar
1 teaspoon salt
Dash of hot pepper sauce

Combine all ingredients in processor or blender and mix until smooth.

Slim Crème Fraîche

Can be refrigerated up to 3 weeks.

Makes about 2 cups

1 pint (2 cups) half and half

1½ tablespoons buttermilk

Combine half and half and buttermilk in glass jar and shake for 1 minute. Let stand in warm place until mixture has thickened (this will take from 4 to 24 hours, depending on the weather).

Artichoke and Fresh Spinach Dressing

Makes about 3 cups

2 8½-ounce cans artichoke hearts, drained and pureed
12 ounces fresh spinach with stems, cooked, squeezed dry and pureed
1 cup mayonnaise (preferably homemade)
¼ cup parsley leaves, minced
2 large shallots, minced
1 large garlic clove, minced

2 tablespoons fresh lemon juice
2 tablespoons freshly snipped chives
2 teaspoons dried dillweed
1 teaspoon salt or to taste
  Freshly ground pepper
  Dash of hot pepper sauce
  Assorted crudités

Combine all ingredients except crudités in food processor or in batches in blender and mix well. Transfer to bowl, cover and chill overnight. Taste and adjust seasoning before serving with assorted crudités.

Sambal Kacang (Java Peanut Dip)

Often used as a hot dressing for vegetable salads in the legendary "Spice Islands."

Makes about 1 cup

½ cup crunchy peanut butter
¼ cup Kecap Manis (see following recipe)
2 tablespoons hot water
1 tablespoon fresh lemon or lime juice

1 teaspoon sugar
1 teaspoon crushed fresh or dried hot red chili
1 garlic clove

Combine all ingredients in processor or blender and puree coarsely, using on/off turns. Transfer to serving bowl. Cover and refrigerate. Bring Sambal Kacang to room temperature before serving.

Kecap Manis (Sweet Soy Sauce)

An Indonesian seasoning that moves easily from Asian to American cooking. It can be purchased at Asian food stores but the homemade variety is infinitely superior and can be refrigerated indefinitely.

Makes about 3 cups

1½ cups sugar
2 cups Chinese soy sauce
¼ cup water
3 to 4 lemongrass stalks (about 10 1-inch pieces) or 1 teaspoon sliced stalks

2 garlic cloves, crushed
2 Chinese star anise

Melt sugar in medium saucepan over low heat until completely dissolved and light caramel color. Gradually stir in soy sauce, water, lemongrass, garlic and star anise, blending well (mixture will bubble over if ingredients are added too quickly). Bring mixture to boil over low heat, stirring constantly, about 10 minutes. Cool 1 hour. Strain through several layers of cheesecloth into jar with tight-fitting lid. Refrigerate sauce until ready to use.

Mustard Seed Vinegar

Useful in marinades, dressings or vinaigrettes.

Makes about 1 quart

2 tablespoons whole mustard seed

1 quart white or cider vinegar

Gently bruise mustard seed, using mortar and pestle. Place in center of 3-inch square of double-thickness cheesecloth and tie with string. Place in tall 1-quart glass bottle. Bring vinegar to simmer, then pour into bottle to fill. Cap and seal. Let stand in cool, dark area for about 10 days to infuse before using.

Greener Goddess Dressing

Greener Goddess Dressing can also be used as a dip for crudités.

Makes about 3 cups

2 cups mayonnaise
½ ripe avocado, mashed
2 large green onions, chopped
¼ cup chopped fresh parsley
¼ cup olive oil
3 tablespoons white wine vinegar

2 tablespoons anchovy paste
1 garlic clove, chopped
1 teaspoon dried tarragon, crumbled
Freshly ground pepper

Combine all ingredients in processor or blender and mix thoroughly. Pour into jar with tight-fitting lid. Refrigerate until ready to serve. Shake well before using.

Walnut Oil Dressing

Makes 4 cups

4 eggs
⅔ cup (about) red wine vinegar
⅓ cup finely minced shallot
1 tablespoon salt
Freshly ground pepper

Juice of 1 lemon
1 cup walnut oil*
1 cup olive oil
⅓ cup finely chopped walnuts
⅓ cup minced fresh parsley

Soft-cook eggs 3 minutes. Drain; let stand until cool enough to handle. Carefully open and add yolks to mixing bowl; finely chop whites. Add ⅓ cup vinegar, shallot, salt, pepper and lemon juice and whisk until thick and frothy. Slowly begin adding oils, whisking constantly until mixture is a medium-thick sauce. Blend in chopped white, nuts and parsley. Stir in remaining vinegar. Taste and adjust seasoning as necessary.

*Walnut oil can be found in specialty shops and some supermarkets. If unavailable, use a total of 2 cups olive oil.

Garlic Oil

Use in salad dressings and marinades.

Makes 1 quart or liter jar

16 garlic cloves, peeled

Olive oil

Thread garlic onto long bamboo skewer. Insert into tall glass 1-quart or 1-liter bottle and fill almost to top with olive oil. Cap. Store in cool, dry area for at least 10 days to infuse before using.

❦ *How to Buy and Use Olive Oil*

Olive oil is the main cooking medium in Central and Southern Italy. You'll want to keep both full- and light-bodied examples on hand.

The finest olive oils are first pressings. After the olives are pressed, the oil is filtered (the amount of filtering determines how full-flavored it will be). The result is fruity-tasting oil. (These oils were formerly labeled "virgin.")

Inferior oils are produced by further pressings of the remaining pits and flesh. These second and third pressings can have an unpleasant, acid aftertaste. They are used in blends with other oils or marketed as "100% olive oil."

The best place to shop for oils is in an Italian grocery or well-stocked gourmet shop. Buy several small containers and sample until you find two that you like.

Store olive oil in a cool, dark spot, not in the refrigerator. Many experts claim that it will keep indefinitely but actually once opened, oil can go rancid in hot weather. Buy only in sizes you can use up within about two months. Unopened oil keeps for up to a year.

Full-Bodied Olive Oil

The aristocrat of the oil world, taken from first pressings with a robust fruity flavor of fresh olives and no acid aftertaste.

What to Look For:

- Green to green-gold color.
- Label stating "first pressing." With Italian oil, look for "Kalamata."
- With French oil (excellent substitute for Italian), look for *"Extra Vierge"* or *"Huile Vierge Première Pression a Froid"* on the label. Both these terms indicate first pressing without heat.

How to Use:

- In hearty sauces, stews, soups or sautés.
- With strong-flavored salad greens—escarole, chicory or arugala.

Light Olive Oil

First pressings, delicate in character, lighter in consistency.

What to Look For:

- Golden color.
- Label stating "first pressing."
- Brands from Lucca, Italy.

How to Use:

- In subtle sauces, stews, soups or sautés.
- With lightly flavored salad greens—romaine, leaf and Bibb lettuces.

Caraway Seed Vinegar

Use in cabbage slaw and sauerbraten.

Makes about 1 quart

2 tablespoons caraway seed

1 quart red wine vinegar or cider vinegar

Gently bruise caraway seed, using mortar and pestle. Place in center of 3-inch square of double-thickness cheesecloth and tie with string. Place in tall 1-quart glass bottle. Bring vinegar to simmer, then pour into bottle to fill. Cap and seal. Let stand in cool, dark area for about 10 days to infuse before using.

Five-Herb Vinegar

Makes 1 gallon

Peel from 2 lemons (without pith)
1 cup fresh mint leaves, loosely packed

1 cup fresh basil leaves, loosely packed
8 to 10 sprigs fresh tarragon

10 sprigs fresh thyme, leaves only
3 small sprigs fresh oregano
4 large garlic cloves, peeled and slivered
4 quarts white wine vinegar

To dry lemon peel and mint: Break peel into 1-inch pieces. Spread on fine-mesh screen over cake rack. Place mint leaves on separate screen. Both ingredients may be set outdoors in a protected but sunny spot so air can circulate. Make sure to bring racks in at night.

Combine peel, herbs and garlic in 1-gallon glass jar or jug that has been scalded with hot water and dried. Heat vinegar just to boiling point and add to jar. Cover tightly and store in dark cupboard 2 weeks, inverting jar occasionally to redistribute ingredients.

Pour vinegar through a paper-filter-lined funnel into small bottles. Cork tightly and store at room temperature.

If drying peel and mint with microwave, allow 8 to 10 minutes for lemon peel and 1½ to 2 minutes for mint, stirring several times.

5 ❧ Main-Course Salads

There was a time—surprisingly, not all that long ago—when the idea of serving a salad for a main course seemed positively bohemian. Fortunately, our meat-and-potatoes culture has changed its outlook enough to realize the nutritional benefits of fresh greens and vegetables tossed or attractively arranged with seafood, poultry or meat. The resulting trend toward lighter fare has been a real boon to the creative cook, for salads not only are the easiest of all main courses to prepare, but the seasonal nature of their ingredients means they rely on what it freshest—and most economical.

Main-course salads have been inspired by cuisine from every corner of the world. From France, for example, comes the classic Salade Niçoise (page 94), as well as suave mustard-spiked Beef and Mushroom Salad (page 102). Orzo Salad with Mussels (page 92) and Chicken and Tubettini in Artichokes (page 99) have a distinctly Italian flair, while Duck Salad with Lichee (page 101) and Sushi Salad (page 95) add a touch of the Orient to a menu. No matter what the choice, simply add a chilled white wine, Beaujolais or rosé to complete the picture. Beer is also an excellent accompaniment to many of the more robust combinations.

Some of these salads, including the Mediterranean-inspired Roasted Pepper Salad with Feta and Shrimp (page 89) and the Crabmeat Salad in Shells (page 86) can be partially prepared ahead for added serving convenience. Remember that many steps in a recipe—poaching poultry or fish, chopping vegetables or making a special dressing—can be done in advance. That leaves assembling the ingredients as the only last-minute chore the busy host or hostess has to worry about.

Use the following recipes to inspire your own creations: Add or subtract basic ingredients according to what is available. The result will be a unique main-course salad that is as healthful as it is delicious.

🍏 Seafood Salads

Crab Salad

4 to 6 servings

1 6½-ounce can crabmeat, well drained
1 cup peeled and finely diced apple
7 ounces finely diced Gouda cheese (about 1 cup)
1 cup finely diced celery
1 cup finely chopped fresh parsley
1 cup finely diced hard-cooked egg
½ cup finely chopped green onion (white part only)

Dressing
1 or 2 egg yolks

1 tablespoon fresh lemon juice
1 teaspoon Dijon mustard
Salt and freshly ground white pepper
½ cup olive oil
½ cup vegetable oil
1 tablespoon catsup
1 tablespoon whiskey

1 hard-cooked egg (garnish)
Parsley sprigs (garnish)

Combine first 7 ingredients in large salad bowl and toss gently to combine. Cover and refrigerate.

For dressing: Combine egg yolks, lemon juice, mustard, salt and pepper in processor or blender and mix well. With machine running, add oils through feed tube or lid, mixing in slow, steady stream until thick and creamy (thin with more lemon juice, if necessary). Mix in catsup and whiskey.

Divide crab mixture evenly among individual plates. Slice egg thinly crosswise. Scallop edges of slices to resemble flower, using small round pastry cutter. Set one atop each salad, using parsley sprigs for leaves and stems. Pour dressing into bowl and pass separately.

Crabmeat Salad in Shells

6 servings

12 hard-shell blue crabs*

½ pound small pasta shells

¼ pound asparagus (trimmed), stems peeled

3 medium tomatoes, peeled, seeded and chopped (about 1 pound)

3 egg yolks, room temperature
1½ tablespoons fresh lemon juice

2½ teaspoons snipped fresh chives
1½ teaspoons Dijon mustard
1½ teaspoons grated lemon peel
1 tablespoon minced fresh tarragon or large pinch dried, crumbled
1 cup plus 2 tablespoons olive oil
6 tablespoons vegetable oil

Watercress sprigs (garnish)

Combine crabs in stockpot with enough cold water to cover. Cover and bring to boil over high heat. Let boil 5 minutes. Drain and cool. Remove legs and body from top shells. Scrub top shells; dry shells and refrigerate until ready to use. Remove meat from legs, claws and bodies. Transfer to bowl.

Bring large amount of salted water to rapid boil. Stir in pasta shells and cook until just tender but firm to the bite (al dente), about 7 to 8 minutes. Drain and pat dry with paper towels. Add pasta shells to crabmeat.

Meanwhile, bring large pot of salted water to rapid boil. Add asparagus and cook until crisp-tender, 2 to 3 minutes. Drain and plunge into cold water to stop cooking process. Drain and dry well. Cut asparagus stalks diagonally into ¾-inch pieces. Add asparagus to crabmeat mixture. Blend in tomato.

Combine egg yolks, lemon juice, chives, mustard, lemon peel and tarragon in processor or blender. With machine running, gradually add olive and vegetable oils in slow, steady stream and mix until thick and creamy. Pour dressing over crabmeat mixture and toss gently. Cover salad and refrigerate for up to 2 hours.

To serve, divide crab salad among reserved shells. Garnish with watercress.

*Two cups cooked flaked King, Dungeness or stone crab can be substituted.

Salad of Scallops and Cucumber

4 servings

6 cups water
1 pound sea scallops, each cut horizontally into 3 slices

2 small cucumbers, scored and cut into 24 rounds
16 inner leaves of romaine lettuce

2 medium tomatoes, sliced
¼ cup minced green onion tops or minced fresh chives
Spanish Sherry wine vinegar
Salt and freshly ground pepper

Bring 6 cups water to gentle simmer in large saucepan over medium-high heat. Add scallops and cook about 3 to 5 seconds. Drain immediately and transfer to bowl of ice water to stop cooking process. Drain again and set aside. *(Can be prepared 1 day ahead to this point, covered and refrigerated.)*

Overlap 6 cucumber slices at top of each plate. Divide scallop slices evenly among plates, arranging between cucumber slices. Place 4 romaine leaves at bottom of each plate and overlap ¼ of tomato slices over top. Sprinkle with onion tops or chives. Drizzle Sherry wine vinegar over all. Sprinkle with salt and pepper to taste and serve.

Shrimp Salad with Mushrooms

8 servings

20 large shrimp, shelled and deveined (tails intact)*
Court bouillon for poaching (about 6 to 8 cups)

16 snow peas

10 large white mushrooms, cleaned and thinly sliced

½ cup chopped unsalted macadamia nuts
3 tablespoons finely minced red onion
Vinaigrette (see following recipe)
8 lettuce leaves

Poach shrimp in gently simmering court bouillon until pink, about 3 minutes. Transfer shrimp to bowl, using slotted spoon (reserve bouillon for another use). Let shrimp cool to room temperature, then refrigerate.

Carefully slice 8 largest shrimp in half lengthwise down through tails. Reserve for garnish. Slice remaining shrimp in medallions crosswise, discarding tails.

Blanch snow peas in boiling salted water for 2 to 3 minutes. Drain well and pat dry with paper towels. Cut each pod diagonally into 3 pieces.

Combine shrimp, snow peas, mushrooms, macadamia nuts and onion in large bowl. Add vinaigrette to taste and toss gently. Arrange lettuce leaves on individual plates. Mound salad in center. Garnish each serving with 2 reserved shrimp halves. Pass any remaining vinaigrette separately.

*One to one and one-half pounds fresh crabmeat can be substituted for shrimp.

Vinaigrette

2 tablespoons Dijon mustard	½ cup (8 tablespoons) olive oil
¼ cup lime juice or to taste	½ cup (8 tablespoons) vegetable or
2 tablespoons chopped fresh dill or	corn oil
2 teaspoons dried dillweed	Salt and freshly ground pepper

Combine mustard and ¼ cup lime juice in small bowl and mix well. Add chopped dill. Add oils 1 tablespoon at a time, whisking well after each addition. Add more lime juice if desired. Season to taste with salt and pepper.

Pasta Shells Stuffed with Shrimp and Cucumber Salad

6 servings

1 small to medium cucumber, peeled, seeded and cut into ¼-inch dice
1 to 2 teaspoons salt
18 giant pasta shells
1 pound medium-size cooked shrimp
⅔ cup whipping cream
2 tablespoons fresh lemon juice
1 tablespoon Dijon mustard

¾ teaspoon salt
⅛ teaspoon freshly ground white pepper
⅔ cup olive oil
1 to 2 tablespoons minced fresh mint leaves

6 long, thin, diagonal slices unpeeled cucumber
Caviar (garnish)

Place cucumber in colander and sprinkle with 1 to 2 teaspoons salt. Drain 30 minutes. Taste cucumber and rinse if too salty. Dry thoroughly with towel.

Bring large amount of salted water to rapid boil. Stir in pasta shells and cook until tender but firm to the bite (al dente), about 12 to 15 minutes. Drain and rinse under cold water. Drain well. Pat dry with paper towels.

Chop shrimp finely. Transfer to large bowl. Add cucumber. Beat cream, lemon juice, mustard, salt and pepper in medium bowl. Whisk in olive oil in slow, steady stream. Stir in mint. Add ½ cup dressing to shrimp-cucumber mixture. Refrigerate remaining dressing. Fill each pasta shell evenly with shrimp mixture. Refrigerate up to 2 hours.

To serve, lay 1 cucumber slice on each plate. Arrange 3 filled pasta shells decoratively over cucumber. Spoon remaining dressing over shells. Garnish each shell with caviar and serve.

Niçoise Vegetable Soup; Provençal Potato Salad

Onion Panade; Tomato Salad with Lentils

Artichoke and Fresh Spinach Dressin

Sambal Kacang (Java Peanut Dip)

Irwin Horowitz

Chicken and Tubettini in Artichokes;
Transparent Noodles with Orange Pork;
Pasta Shells Stuffed with Shrimp and Cucumber Salad;
Lasagne Spinach Rolls with Gorgonzola Dressing;
Crabmeat Salad in Shells

lade Niçoise

Soufflé-Stuffed Artichoke;
Tomato Filled with Curried Salmon Salad

Japanese Summer Salad

6 servings

½ pound flat Japanese noodles (udon) or linguine (broken in half)
1 pound cooked small shrimp
1 bunch green onions, thinly sliced

¼ cup sesame oil mixed with ¼ cup peanut oil
½ pound button mushrooms, sliced
⅓ to ½ cup Japanese soy sauce

¼ cup saké
¼ cup toasted sesame seed
2 tablespoons grated fresh ginger
2 garlic cloves, mashed

3 eggs
½ teaspoon salt
1 tablespoon coarsely crumbled nori (dried laver or seaweed)

Bring large amount of salted water to rapid boil. Stir in noodles and cook until just tender but firm to the bite (al dente), about 10 minutes. Drain and rinse under cold water. Drain and pat dry with paper towels. Transfer noodles to large bowl. Add shrimp and green onion and mix well.

Heat 2 tablespoons oil mixture in large skillet over medium-high heat. Add mushrooms and sauté 5 minutes. Add to shrimp mixture. Blend in soy sauce, saké, sesame seed, ginger, garlic and remaining oil mixture. Cover and refrigerate for up to 2 hours.

Beat eggs with salt in small bowl. Stir in nori. Lightly oil heavy 8-inch skillet. Place skillet over medium-high heat, add about ¼ cup egg mixture and cook until crepe loosens from pan when lightly shaken. Turn crepe over, cook briefly, then slide onto work surface. Repeat twice for a total of 3 crepes. Cool completely. Roll crepes up and slice rolls crosswise to form thin shreds.

Toss noodle mixture gently to reblend. Spoon evenly into individual bowls. Top with crepe shreds. Set bowls in crushed ice and serve.

Roasted Pepper Salad with Feta and Shrimp

A perfect main course for summer. Serve with country bread, a fruity white wine and an iced fruit soufflé.

4 to 6 servings

1 cup plain yogurt
5 fresh mint leaves or ½ teaspoon dried, crumbled
1 small garlic clove, chopped

3 green bell peppers, rinsed and dried
3 sweet red bell peppers, rinsed and dried
2 yellow sweet peppers,* rinsed and dried

1 tablespoon olive oil
1 tablespoon wine vinegar

8 inner leaves of romaine lettuce
1 pound jumbo shrimp, cooked, peeled and deveined
½ pound feta or fresh goat cheese, coarsely crumbled
½ cup Greek olives
3 small green onions, shredded

Combine yogurt, mint and garlic in processor or blender and puree.

Preheat broiler. Pierce each pepper near stem with sharp, thin knife. Arrange peppers on broiler pan and roast on all sides until blistered (but not charred). Transfer to plastic or paper bag, close tightly and set aside for 15 minutes. Slip off skins; discard stems and seeds. Slice peppers into thin strips. Transfer to large bowl. Add olive oil and vinegar and toss gently until blended.

Arrange romaine leaves in fan pattern on serving platter. Mound peppers in center. Drizzle some yogurt dressing over top. Scatter shrimp, cheese, olives and green onion around peppers. Cover and chill slightly before serving with remaining dressing.

*If unavailable, substitute 1 additional green and 1 additional red pepper.

❦ Classic Mayonnaise

Mayonnaise is a cold sauce of eggs, oil and seasonings blended into an emulsion. Excellent in its own right as a dressing or a spread, mayonnaise is the basis of many other cold sauces—such as Russian Dressing, Tartar Sauce, Sauce Rémoulade—that enhance the flavor of fish, fowl, meat, shellfish and raw or cooked vegetables.

Why make your own mayonnaise, when it is so readily available commercially? Quite simply, because the flavor of homemade mayonnaise is incomparable. And it's easy to make. Although mayonnaise is traditionally whisked by hand, the following recipe can be whipped up in short order with an electric mixer. With the help of a blender or food processor, it takes even less time.

Properly stabilized, your mayonnaise will remain fresh and creamy in the refrigerator for at least a week.

Classic Mayonnaise

All ingredients should be at room temperature or slightly warm.

If homemade mayonnaise is to be stored for more than a day or so, it must be stabilized to prevent separating. For each cup of completed mayonnaise, beat in 2 teaspoons boiling water or stock (chicken or beef).

Makes about 1½ cups

2 egg yolks*
1 teaspoon Dijon mustard or more to taste
1 tablespoon tarragon or wine vinegar or lemon juice
⅓ cup olive oil
⅔ cup peanut oil
Salt and white pepper

Mixer or Whisk Method: Place yolks, mustard and vinegar in a large bowl and beat 1 minute. Add half the oil *very slowly,* drop by drop, beating vigorously and constantly (if oil is added too rapidly, yolks will not completely absorb the oil and the mayonnaise will have a runny consistency). You may add remaining oil by teaspoonfuls, beating constantly. Add salt and white pepper to taste.

Blender or Food Processor Method: Place yolks, mustard, vinegar, salt and pepper in blender, or food processor equipped with steel blade. Turn motor on and immediately begin adding oil in a thin stream. When all oil has been added and mixture has thickened, turn off the machine.

*If using food processor method, 2 whole eggs can be substituted for 2 egg yolks. This will produce a slightly less stiff mayonnaise.

Great Hints

• If you are following the mixer/whisk method, use a bulb baster for the drop-by-drop addition of oil; it's much easier than trying to pour droplets with one hand while mixing with the other.

• Three techniques for salvaging separated mayonnaise:

1. Put 1 tablespoon mayonnaise into a warm, dry bowl with 1 teaspoon prepared mustard. Whip until creamy. Add remaining mayonnaise a tablespoon at a time, beating vigorously after each addition.

2. Substitute 1 tablespoon boiling water for mustard; follow same procedure as above.

3. Place a fresh egg yolk in bowl. Beat in separated mixture plus ½ cup oil to balance extra yolk.

- Store homemade mayonnaise in refrigerator, covering surface with plastic wrap to prevent discoloration.

- The balance of oil can be adjusted to suit individual tastes. Although the ratio of ⅔ cup peanut oil to ⅓ cup olive oil is a good one, you may prefer to use more or less olive oil, or, if serving the mayonnaise with delicately flavored food, to eliminate the olive oil altogether. Vegetable oil can also be substituted for either olive or peanut oil.

Variations
For one cup mayonnaise:

- *Russian Dressing:* Whisk in a tablespoon (or more to taste) catsup or chili sauce. Serve with fresh salad greens.

- *Tartar Sauce:* Add finely chopped gherkins or dill pickles, parsley and onion. Good with poached or fried fish.

- *Mustard Sauce:* Add additional Dijon mustard to taste. Serve with shellfish.

- *Garlic Sauce (Aïoli):* Add 2 minced garlic cloves or more to taste.

- *Shallot Sauce:* Add 1 tablespoon minced shallots or to taste.

- *Rémoulade Sauce:* Mix in small amounts of anchovy paste, minced gherkins, capers, chopped parsley, chervil and tarragon. Serve with cold meats, chicken, sliced hard-cooked eggs.

- *Roquefort Cream:* Mix with ½ cup whipped cream and ¼ cup crumbled Roquefort cheese. Serve with lettuce hearts or any other salad greens.

- *Andalouse Sauce:* Add ¼ cup tomato puree, ½ chopped sweet red pepper and 1 teaspoon each tarragon and chopped chives. Serve with cold chicken.

- *Maltaise Sauce:* Whisk in ¼ cup fresh orange juice and finely grated orange peel to taste. Good with cooked carrots or cauliflower.

- *Lemon Sauce:* Add fresh lemon juice to taste. Good with cold artichokes and asparagus.

Warm Green Salad with Mussels

4 servings

 1 small head Boston lettuce
32 leaves of arugula or other tangy green
 1 head red leaf lettuce
24 mussels, debearded and well scrubbed
 1 25.4-ounce bottle dry white wine
 2 cups fish fumet or clam juice

 1 medium carrot, finely diced
 1 small onion, finely diced
 1 cup whipping cream
 2 to 3 saffron threads
 1 tomato, peeled, seeded and cut into small dice (garnish)
 ½ cup celery, cut into fine julienne (garnish)

Divide Boston lettuce, arugula and red leaf lettuce among 4 large shallow bowls or rimmed plates. Combine mussels and wine in large saucepan or Dutch oven over medium-high heat. Cover and cook until mussels open, about 3 to 4 minutes. Discard any unopened mussels.

Strain cooking liquid into large saucepan, removing any shell. Remove mussels from shells and keep warm over simmering water. Add fumet, carrot and onion to cooking liquid and cook over medium-high heat until reduced by half, about 30 minutes. Reduce heat, stir in cream and saffron and simmer, stirring constantly, until sauce is smooth, about 20 minutes. Arrange 6 mussels over each salad, then top with some of sauce. Garnish with diced tomato and celery julienne.

Orzo Salad with Mussels

6 servings

30 large mussels, scrubbed and debearded*
⅓ cup dry white wine
 2 shallots, minced

½ cup orzo (rice-shaped pasta)
⅓ cup chopped celery leaves
¼ cup *each* minced red and green bell pepper
¼ cup chopped watercress

1½ teaspoons fresh lemon juice
 1 teaspoon sugar
 ½ teaspoon dry mustard
 ¼ teaspoon celery seed
 ⅓ cup olive oil
 Salt

 6 slices crisply cooked bacon, crumbled

Combine mussels, wine and shallot in large skillet and bring to boil over medium-high heat. Reduce heat to low, cover and simmer, removing mussels from skillet with a slotted spoon as shells open, about 10 to 15 minutes; discard any that do not open. Reserve 2 tablespoons liquid. Set aside to cool.

Bring large amount of salted water to rapid boil. Stir in orzo and cook until just tender but firm to the bite (al dente), about 10 to 12 minutes. Drain and rinse under cold water. Drain well and pat dry with paper towels. Transfer to large bowl. Add celery leaves, peppers and watercress and blend thoroughly.

Combine reserved mussel liquid, lemon juice, sugar, mustard and celery seed in small bowl. Whisk in olive oil 1 drop at a time. Taste and season with salt as desired. Pour dressing over orzo mixture and toss gently.

Open mussels and loosen from shell. Discard top shells. Top each mussel in shell with 1 tablespoon orzo mixture. Arrange on platter. Refrigerate up to 2 hours. Sprinkle crumbled bacon evenly over mussels and serve.

* Oysters can be substituted for mussels.

Smoked Salmon in Artichokes

2 servings

2 large artichokes
1 lemon, halved
1 tablespoon all purpose flour
2 cups water

2 ounces smoked salmon, minced
2 tablespoons mayonnaise (preferably homemade)
2 tablespoons sour cream

1 tablespoon minced fresh parsley
1 teaspoon minced onion
1 teaspoon minced capers, rinsed and drained
Lettuce leaves
Cherry tomato slices or pimiento strips (garnish)

Trim stem from artichokes; remove tough outer leaves and cut off top third. Trim tips of leaves with scissors or kitchen shears. Rub cut surfaces with ½ lemon. Remove chokes, using serrated spoon. Sift flour into 2-quart saucepan. Add water and whisk until flour is dissolved. Squeeze remaining lemon into pan and blend well. Add artichokes. Bring to boil over medium-high heat. Reduce heat, cover and simmer until artichokes are tender, about 30 minutes. Drain well. Cover and refrigerate until ready to use.

Combine salmon, mayonnaise, sour cream, parsley, onion and capers in small bowl and mix well. Spoon into artichokes. Arrange lettuce leaves on plates and set artichokes on top. Garnish with tomato or pimiento.

Tomatoes Filled with Curried Salmon Salad

Begin with chilled avocado soup and pass a basket of thinly sliced buttered whole wheat toast with the toma-toes for a light lunch. Open a bottle of Fumé Blanc or Sauvignon Blanc.

4 to 6 servings

¾ cup mayonnaise
6 tablespoons fresh lime juice
6 tablespoons chopped chutney
½ to 1 teaspoon curry powder or to taste
Salt and freshly ground pepper
2 cups flaked cooked salmon
1 medium cucumber, peeled and chopped

1 green onion, chopped
2 tablespoons minced fresh parsley

4 to 6 large tomatoes
Lettuce leaves
Lemon wedges and mint sprigs (garnish)

Combine mayonnaise, lime juice, chutney, curry, salt and pepper in small bowl. Mix salmon, cucumber, onion and parsley in another bowl and toss gently with ⅓ of mayonnaise mixture.

Cut out stem end and remove core from tomatoes. Cut each tomato in eighths, *but do not slice through.* Gently open sections to form flowerlike container. Fill with salmon salad. Place on lettuce-lined plates and garnish with lemon wedges and mint sprigs. Pass remaining curried mayonnaise separately.

Smoked Trout Salad

6 servings

2 cups hickory chips
2 pounds fresh trout (about 4 small), cleaned but not boned

1 pound green beans

Escarole leaves

1 bunch radishes, shredded
2 large tomatoes, peeled, seeded and chopped
Chuck's Special Dressing (see recipe, page 76)

Soak hickory chips in water 20 minutes. Arrange in bottom of electric smoker.*
Place tray half filled with water over chips. Set trout on grill, cover and smoke 1

hour; do not remove lid while cooking. *(Procedure may vary with manufacturer's instructions. Trout can be refrigerated up to 2 weeks after cooking in smoker.)*

Transfer trout to work surface. Remove skin, bone carefully and cut fish into narrow strips. Wrap fish tightly in foil and refrigerate until ready to use.

French cut beans. Blanch in boiling salted water until crisp-tender, about 2 minutes. Plunge into cold water to stop cooking process. Drain beans well; gently pat dry with paper towels.

Cover serving platter with escarole leaves. Place beans down center of platter. Arrange trout in lengthwise strip over beans. Place narrow strip of radish on each side of beans. Arrange tomato at top and bottom of platter. Refrigerate at least 1 hour. (If salad has been chilled over 3 hours, let stand at room temperature 15 minutes before serving.) Serve immediately with Chuck's Special Dressing.

*If commercial smoker is not available, soak 2 cups hickory chips in water 20 minutes. Meanwhile, line very heavy skillet or lidded casserole with heavy-duty aluminum foil, bringing enough foil up above rim so it will completely cover lid and form tight seal. Arrange hickory chips in single layer in bottom of skillet. Sprinkle 1 tablespoon sugar over chips. Set rack about 2 to 3 inches above chips. Generously butter rack. Arrange trout on rack and cover skillet with lid. Bring foil up over lid, folding and pleating to make tight seal. Smoke fish over high heat 20 minutes; do not overcook.

For variation, poach trout in fish fumet or court bouillon; do not overcook.

Salade du Sud

4 servings

1 10-ounce can tuna, drained and flaked
1 cup cooked brown rice, chilled
½ cup Italian salad dressing
1 large tomato, cut into wedges
½ cup thinly sliced green onion
½ green pepper, seeded and chopped
Salt and freshly ground pepper
4 hard-cooked eggs, shelled and sliced
Sesame crackers

Combine tuna, rice and dressing in medium bowl and mix well. Blend in tomato, onion and green pepper. Season to taste with salt and pepper. Cover and refrigerate. To serve, mound salad in center of platter and arrange egg slices over top. Serve with crackers.

Salade Niçoise

6 servings

¾ pound fresh green beans, cut into thirds
1 teaspoon salt

1 7-ounce can tuna packed in oil, drained and flaked
Vinaigrette (see following recipe)
1 small or ½ large cucumber, peeled and thinly sliced
10 to 12 anchovy fillets, soaked in milk, drained and split lengthwise
¼ cup Italian black olives or Greek olives, halved and pitted
3 medium tomatoes, peeled, seeded and cut into quarters

Add green beans and salt to 1 quart rapidly boiling water. Return to boil and cook beans until just tender, about 15 minutes. Transfer to very cold water, using slotted spoon, and let cool completely. Drain thoroughly.

Place tuna in shallow serving dish or salad bowl. Cover with green beans and moisten with some of vinaigrette. Overlap cucumber slices to cover beans. Spoon vinaigrette over, reserving only a small amount. Arrange anchovies in lattice pattern over cucumbers. Put olive halves, rounded side up, in center of each lattice. Arrange tomato around edge of salad and brush with remaining vinaigrette. Cover and chill up to 8 hours before serving.

Vinaigrette

2 tablespoons fresh lemon juice	Salt and freshly ground pepper
1 garlic clove, crushed	6 tablespoons olive oil

Combine lemon juice, garlic, salt and pepper in small bowl. Whisk in olive oil.

Sushi Salad

6 servings

Rice

1 cup medium- or short-grain white rice
1½ cups water
1 tablespoon Mirin
½ teaspoon salt

¼ cup rice vinegar
2 teaspoons sugar
½ teaspoon salt

Garnish
½ cup water
1 tablespoon soy sauce
1 teaspoon sugar
½ carrot, cut julienne

⅓ cup canned bamboo shoots, cut julienne
½ cucumber, peeled, seeded and thinly sliced
20 snow peas, blanched and sliced
1 green onion (including 3 inches green top), thinly sliced
8 ounces fresh uncooked tuna, sole or cooked shrimp, cut into thin strips (about 2¼ inches), chilled

Dipping Sauce (optional)
½ cup soy sauce
3 tablespoons rice vinegar

For rice: Place rice in strainer and wash well under cold running water about 2 minutes. Let rice drain about 30 minutes. Combine rice, water, Mirin and salt in heavy 2-quart saucepan and bring to boil over high heat. Reduce heat, cover and simmer about 15 minutes, stirring occasionally to prevent sticking. Remove from heat and let stand, covered, about 5 minutes.

Mix rice vinegar, sugar and salt in small saucepan and bring to boil. Remove from heat. Transfer rice to nonaluminum shallow dish. Slowly pour hot vinegar mixture over rice and toss with fork (fan rice with other hand as you blend to make rice glisten). Cover with damp cloth. Let stand at room temperature until ready to use.

For garnish: Bring water, soy sauce and sugar to boil in small saucepan. Add carrot and cook 3 minutes. Stir in bamboo shoots and cook until crisp-tender, about 1 minute. Drain and let stand at room temperature until cool.

Divide rice among 6 serving bowls. Sprinkle carrot, bamboo shoots, cucumber, snow peas and green onion over top. Arrange fish in center.

For dipping sauce: Blend soy sauce and rice vinegar in bowl. Pass separately.

Cold Snapper and Pasta Salad

6 to 8 servings

1 pound red snapper
2 to 3 tablespoons butter
1 green pepper, chopped
1 zucchini, sliced
½ pound mushrooms, sliced
½ pound snow peas

½ red onion, chopped
1 pound spaghettini, cooked al dente and drained
Herb Dressing (see recipe, page 97)

Preheat oven to 400°F. Arrange fish in baking dish. Sprinkle with small amount of water. Bake until fish is flaky and tender, about 15 minutes. Meanwhile, melt butter in large skillet over medium-high heat. Add green pepper, zucchini, mushrooms, snow peas and onion and sauté until crisp-tender, 5 minutes. Cut fish into small pieces. Transfer to large bowl. Add vegetables and pasta. Add enough Herb Dressing to moisten and toss well. Cover and chill at least 30 minutes.

🍂 Poultry Salads

Chicken Salad

4 to 6 servings

3 cups diced cooked chicken
3 tablespoons fresh lemon juice

1 cup mayonnaise
1 teaspoon salt
1 teaspoon dry mustard

1 teaspoon curry powder
1½ cups seedless grapes
1 cup drained pineapple tidbits
½ cup slivered almonds, toasted
¼ cup water chestnuts, diced

Toss chicken with lemon juice in large bowl. Cover and refrigerate 1 hour.

Combine next 4 ingredients in small bowl. Add remaining ingredients to chicken and toss lightly. Blend in mayonnaise mixture.

Cold Lemon Chicken Salad

4 servings

1 3- to 3½-pound whole chicken
3 cups water
½ onion
1 carrot
1 garlic clove
Parsley sprigs
Salt and freshly ground pepper

2 cups fresh bean sprouts
Boiling water

2 eggs, beaten

Lemon Dressing
1 cup broth from chicken

2 tablespoons sugar or to taste
1 teaspoon cornstarch
Finely grated peel and juice of 3 lemons
Salt and freshly ground white pepper

2 cups drained canned bamboo shoots, shredded
2 green onions, thinly sliced (garnish)
2 lemons, halved lengthwise and cut into thin half-moon slices (garnish)

Combine first 6 ingredients with salt and pepper in large saucepan. Cover and bring to boil; reduce heat and simmer until cooked through, about 45 minutes. Remove chicken and set aside to cool. Strain broth, reserving 1 cup for dressing. Discard skin and bones from chicken; shred meat and set aside.

Place bean sprouts in colander and pour boiling water over; rinse quickly in cold water and drain well.

Pour eggs into 8-inch pan and make thin omelet. Turn out of pan, cool slightly and cut into shreds.

For dressing: Combine all ingredients in small saucepan and simmer over low heat, stirring frequently, until slightly thickened. Set aside to cool.

To serve, combine chicken, bean sprouts, omelet shreds, dressing and bamboo shoots in large bowl and toss thoroughly. Arrange in center of platter. Sprinkle with onion and surround with lemon slices.

Chicken and Grape Salad

4 servings

2 cooked whole chicken breasts, boned, skinned and diced
4 celery stalks, diced
½ cup slivered almonds, toasted
½ cup sliced seedless green grapes
1 teaspoon fresh lemon juice
  Mayonnaise
  Salt and freshly ground pepper
  Romaine lettuce leaves

1 bunch spinach leaves
2 carrots, thinly sliced
1 cucumber, peeled and sliced
1 cup alfalfa sprouts
4 green onions, diced
  Chilled cooked asparagus (garnish)
  Herb Dressing (optional) (see following recipe)

Combine chicken, celery, almonds, grapes and lemon juice in small bowl. Add enough mayonnaise to moisten and mix well. Season with salt and pepper. Cover and refrigerate until ready to use. Line 4 individual plates with lettuce and spinach leaves. Arrange carrot, cucumber, alfalfa sprouts and onion around edges. Mound chicken mixture in center. Top with asparagus. Pass dressing separately, if desired.

Herb Dressing

Makes about 2 cups

1⅓ cups oil
¼ cup plus 2 tablespoons white wine vinegar
2 tablespoons minced fresh chives
2 tablespoons minced fresh parsley
2 garlic cloves, minced
1 teaspoon dried basil, crumbled
1 teaspoon salt

½ teaspoon dry mustard
½ teaspoon dried oregano, crumbled
½ teaspoon dried tarragon, crumbled
¼ teaspoon freshly ground pepper
  Ground red pepper to taste

Combine all ingredients in jar with tight-fitting lid and shake well. Refrigerate until ready to use.

Cubed Chicken in Lettuce Leaves

Preparation time will be reduced if all chopping is done in a processor.

6 servings

1 large chicken breast (about 1 pound), boned, sliced and cut into tiny cubes (about 2 cups)
1 egg white
2 tablespoons cornstarch
½ teaspoon salt

2 long green chilies (hot or mild), cored, seeded and cut into small cubes (about ½ cup)
10 to 12 water chestnuts, cut into small cubes (about ½ cup)
½ cup finely diced celery
3 tablespoons finely diced carrot
1 teaspoon chopped fresh ginger

3 tablespoons finely chopped green onion
2 teaspoons finely chopped garlic
2 tablespoons Shaohsing rice wine* or dry Sherry
1½ teaspoons soy sauce
1½ teaspoons chili paste with garlic*
1 teaspoon sugar
1 tablespoon water

2 cups peanut oil

½ teaspoon sesame oil

1 head iceberg lettuce, cored, leaves separated

Combine chicken, egg white, 1 tablespoon cornstarch and salt in medium bowl and stir to blend well. Cover with plastic and refrigerate at least 30 minutes.

Combine chilies, water chestnuts, celery, carrot and ginger in another bowl. Combine green onion and garlic in separate bowl. Mix wine, soy sauce, chili paste and sugar in another bowl. Blend remaining 1 tablespoon cornstarch and water in small bowl, mixing until smooth.

Pour peanut oil into wok. Place over high heat. When oil begins to smoke, add chicken in batches and cook, stirring to separate cubes, about 1½ minutes. Remove chicken with slotted spoon. Drain well on paper towels and set aside.

Pour off all but 2 tablespoons peanut oil from wok. Return to high heat. Add water chestnut mixture and cook, stirring constantly, about 30 seconds. Add green onion and garlic and cook, stirring constantly, about 10 seconds. Return chicken to wok and cook, stirring constantly, until hot, about 30 seconds. Add wine mixture and sesame oil. Restir dissolved cornstarch. Add to wok and cook, stirring constantly, about 30 seconds. Transfer to heated platter. Spoon chicken mixture into lettuce leaves and fold over to enclose. Serve hot.

* Available in oriental markets.

Chicken Salad with Fried Rice Nests

The contrast of warm crackling bits of fried rice with cool chicken salad is as surprising as it is delicious.

4 servings

Chicken Salad
1¼ pounds boneless chicken breasts
6 tablespoons fresh lime juice
1 cup water or chicken stock
1 teaspoon salt
½ teaspoon freshly ground white pepper

4 green onions (including tops), minced
3 tablespoons minced green or red bell pepper
½ cup mayonnaise (preferably homemade)

Rice Nests
1¼ cups water

2 tablespoons minced onion
1 tablespoon butter
½ teaspoon salt
½ cup long-grain brown rice

2 egg yolks
2 tablespoons whipping cream
½ teaspoon freshly ground white pepper

Peanut oil for deep frying

1 tablespoon minced green bell pepper (garnish)
Watercress and Boston lettuce (garnish)

For salad: Combine chicken breasts and 5 tablespoons lime juice in 9-inch skillet. Cover with water or stock. Sprinkle with ½ teaspoon salt and ¼ teaspoon pepper. Place over medium heat and bring to boil slowly. Reduce heat and simmer for 1 minute. Remove from heat, cover and let stand 20 minutes.

Remove chicken from liquid. Trim off excess fat and pat dry. Shred chicken into 1½ × ½-inch pieces.

Combine onion, bell pepper, mayonnaise and remaining lime juice, salt and pepper in large bowl. Add chicken and toss well. Salad may seem a bit spicy, but chilling will cause seasoning to be absorbed. Cover and refrigerate about 4 hours.

For rice nests: Combine water, onion, butter and salt in heavy 3-quart saucepan over high heat and bring to rolling boil. Stir in rice. Reduce heat, cover and simmer until rice is tender, stirring occasionally to prevent sticking, about 40 minutes. Remove from heat.

Combine egg yolks, cream and pepper in small bowl and stir with fork until blended. Add to rice. Return saucepan to low heat. Beat rice vigorously with wooden spoon until rice thickens and eggs coagulate, about 30 seconds. Remove from heat and continue beating another 30 seconds to cool. Spread rice in shallow baking pan. Cover loosely with plastic and chill thoroughly.

Preheat oven to 250°F. Pour enough oil into large heavy saucepan or electric fryer to fill halfway. Heat to 375°F. Carefully add large spoonfuls of rice (oil will bubble up rapidly) and fry nests on both sides until golden. Remove with slotted spoon and transfer to rack set over baking sheet. Keep rice nests warm in oven.

Arrange chicken salad in center of large serving platter and surround with rice nests. Garnish with green pepper, watercress and Boston lettuce.

Chicken and Tubettini in Artichokes

6 servings

2 pounds tomatoes, peeled, seeded, juiced and chopped
1 tablespoon salt
6 large artichokes
Juice of 1 lemon

¼ pound fresh green beans
¼ pound tubettini noodles (about ½ cup)
3 cups cooked chicken, cut into ½-inch cubes

4 egg yolks
3 to 4 tablespoons fresh lemon juice
1½ cups olive oil
Salt and freshly ground pepper
1½ cups tightly packed fresh basil leaves, minced

2 tablespoons snipped fresh chives (garnish)

Place tomato in colander and sprinkle with salt. Drain 1 hour. Meanwhile, cut 1 inch from top of artichokes. Trim stems and leaf tips. Transfer artichokes to large saucepan. Add juice of 1 lemon and enough water to cover. Cover and simmer until bottoms are tender when pierced with fork, about 20 to 25 minutes. Invert artichokes on paper towels to drain.

Bring large amount of salted water to rapid boil. Add beans and cook until crisp-tender, about 3 to 4 minutes. Drain and rinse under cold water. Drain and pat dry with paper towels. Slice diagonally into ¼-inch pieces. Transfer to large bowl. Bring large amount of salted water to rapid boil. Stir in tubettini and cook until just tender but firm to the bite (al dente), about 8 to 10 minutes. Drain and rinse thoroughly under cold water. Drain and pat dry with paper towels. Add tubettini to beans. Blend in chicken.

Pat tomato dry with paper towels; squeeze dry. Transfer to processor or blender. Add egg yolks and lemon juice and mix well. With machine running, gradually add oil through feed tube and mix until thick and creamy. Season with salt and pepper to taste. Fold in basil. Pour 2 cups dressing over chicken mixture and toss gently. Refrigerate for up to 2 hours.

To serve, remove spiny center leaves and fuzzy choke from artichokes, using spoon. Fill center of artichokes with chicken mixture. Sprinkle with chives. Pass remaining dressing separately.

Warm Chicken and Walnut Salad

6 servings

3 cups chicken stock
3 whole unskinned chicken breasts, boned

1 cup walnut halves and pieces
3 tablespoons light soy sauce
2½ cups cooked long-grain rice, room temperature
¼ cup corn or peanut oil

2 tablespoons vegetable oil
2 tablespoons rice vinegar
Grated peel of 1 lemon

1 tablespoon freshly grated ginger
Lettuce leaves
Seeded red grapes or mandarin orange slices (optional garnish)

Bring chicken stock to boil in medium saucepan. Add chicken, reduce heat and simmer gently until chicken is tender, 10 to 15 minutes. Transfer chicken to work surface; discard skin. Chop chicken into bite-size pieces. Transfer to large bowl.

Preheat oven to 400°F. Line baking sheet with foil. Combine nuts and soy sauce in small bowl and toss to coat well. Arrange in single layer on prepared sheet. Bake until crisp, turning once, about 7 to 8 minutes. Reserve ¼ cup nuts for garnish. Add remainder to chicken. Blend in rice and toss lightly. Combine corn or peanut oil, vegetable oil, rice vinegar and lemon peel in small jar and shake to blend well.

Just before serving, sprinkle ginger over chicken mixture and toss well. Add dressing and toss gently. Spoon salad into lettuce-lined plates. Top with remaining walnut halves and garnish with grapes or mandarin orange slices, if desired.

Chilled Duck Salad

Duck makes this salad especially distinctive, but it's also good made with cold turkey. Try it with English muffins split and spread with curry-flavored mayonnaise and broiled. Serve with a Beaujolais or California Zinfandel.

4 servings

3 cups cold roast duck, skinned and cut into bite-size pieces
3 green onions, chopped
½ green pepper, chopped
½ pound mushrooms, sliced
¼ cup sliced stuffed green olives

Dressing
3 tablespoons red wine vinegar
6 tablespoons olive oil

1 garlic clove, mashed
¼ teaspoon dry mustard
Salt and pepper
Lettuce
Pimiento strips (optional)

Combine duck, onion, green pepper, mushrooms and olives in large bowl.

Combine ingredients for dressing in small bowl and whisk until slightly thickened. Pour dressing over salad mixture and toss to coast lightly. Mound salad on individual lettuce-lined plates and garnish with crossed strips of pimiento, if desired.

Duck and Orange Salad with Pecans

2 servings

2 duck legs and thighs, trimmed
2 teaspoons fresh lemon juice
1 teaspoon minced fresh tarragon or ¼ teaspoon dried, crumbled
1 teaspoon minced fresh parsley
Salt and freshly ground pepper

¼ cup minced green onion (about 3)
3 tablespoons olive oil

1½ tablespoons fresh lemon juice
Grated peel of 1 orange

1 tablespoon butter
1 garlic clove, unpeeled
¼ cup coarsely chopped pecans

1 medium orange, peeled, thinly sliced and seeded
Lettuce leaves

Arrange duck in shallow pan. Combine 2 teaspoons lemon juice with tarragon, parsley, salt and pepper in small bowl. Brush over duck. Let stand at room temperature 1 hour.

Preheat broiler. Place duck in broiling pan and broil until browned and crisp, turning once, about 5 minutes per side. Let cool completely.

Cut meat into strips; discard bones (or use in stock). Combine duck and onion in medium bowl. Whisk olive oil, remaining lemon juice, orange peel and salt and pepper to taste in small bowl. Pour over duck. Refrigerate at least 2 hours, stirring occasionally.

Meanwhile, melt butter in small skillet. Add garlic and cook over low heat 1 to 2 minutes. Discard garlic. Add pecans to skillet and cook until browned and crisp, stirring frequently. Remove from heat and set aside.

When ready to serve, add orange slices to duck and toss well. Taste and adjust seasonings. Arrange lettuce leaves on plates and spoon salad over. Sprinkle with pecans and serve.

Duck Salad with Lichee

2 servings

1 5-pound duck*

½ head lettuce, shredded

Pineapple Dressing
⅔ cup drained canned crushed pineapple
½ cup white vinegar

3 tablespoons vegetable oil
3 tablespoons finely chopped onion
1 to 2 teaspoons curry powder or to taste
Salt
1 20-ounce can lichee nuts

Preheat oven to 350°F. Roast duck, pricking skin frequently to allow fat to drain, until cooked through, about 1¼ hours. Let cool slightly. Discard skin and bone and cut meat into thick slices.

Line platter with shredded lettuce and arrange duck slices over top.

Combine next 6 ingredients for dressing and blend well. Spoon over duck and lettuce. Ring platter with lichee nuts. Serve at room temperature.

*Roast duck is frequently available in oriental markets and can be substituted. Cooked turkey can also be used.

❦ Meat Salads

Chef's Salad

4 servings

1 cup julienne turkey, chicken, beef, ham or tongue, trimmed of all fat
¼ to ⅓ cup thinly sliced onion
⅓ cup robust vinaigrette
1 quart assorted salad greens, torn into pieces
1 cup Swiss cheese, cut julienne
½ cup sliced cucumber (optional)

½ green pepper, cut julienne (optional)
4 artichoke hearts, halved (optional)
4 radishes, sliced (optional)
1 cup croutons (optional)
2 tomatoes, quartered

Place meat and onion in shallow dish. Add vinaigrette and marinate at room temperature 2 hours. Drain and transfer vinaigrette to salad bowl. Place greens over vinaigrette. Add meat, onion and cheese and desired optional ingredients except croutons. Just before serving, add croutons, if desired, and toss. Place tomato around rim of bowl. Serve on chilled plates.

French Beef and Mushroom Salad

2 servings

¼ cup olive oil
1½ tablespoons white wine vinegar
2 teaspoons capers, rinsed, drained and minced
2 teaspoons minced fresh parsley
1 teaspoon Dijon mustard
¼ teaspoon chopped fresh tarragon
Salt and freshly ground pepper
½ pound (about) chilled cooked flank steak, cut into matchstick strips

¼ pound mushrooms, stemmed and sliced

Lettuce leaves
Tomato wedges, stuffed eggs, olives, cornichons or tiny dill pickles (optional garnish)

Combine first 6 ingredients with salt and pepper to taste in mixing bowl and blend well. Add beef and mushrooms and toss to coat thoroughly. Cover and marinate 1 hour at room temperature.

Line plates with lettuce leaves and divide salad evenly. Garnish as desired.

Transparent Noodles with Orange Pork

6 servings

1 pound lean ground pork
¼ cup chopped water chestnuts
1 egg
1 tablespoon grated fresh ginger
1 garlic clove, chopped
1 teaspoon salt
¼ teaspoon freshly ground pepper

¼ cup peanut oil
2 to 4 dried whole red chilies, chopped
Peel of 1 navel orange, cut into ¼ × ½-inch julienne, blanched 7 minutes and drained

1 bunch green onions, cut diagonally into 1-inch pieces

½ pound transparent (cellophane) noodles (dried bean threads)

½ cup hoisin sauce
½ cup peanut oil
¼ cup Japanese soy sauce

Peanut oil
6 egg roll wrappers

Combine pork, water chestnuts, egg, ginger, garlic, salt and pepper in large bowl and mix until thoroughly blended. Shape into ½-inch balls.

Heat ¼ cup peanut oil in large skillet over medium-high heat. Add chilies and orange peel and sauté 1 minute. Remove orange peel from skillet, using slotted spoon. Add pork and cook until meat is no longer pink, turning occasionally. Remove chilies and pork from skillet with slotted spoon. Transfer to large bowl. Add onion and reserved orange peel. Set aside.

Pour enough boiling water over noodles to cover. Let stand 20 minutes. Drain and rinse under cold water. Drain well and pat dry. Add noodles to pork mixture and toss lightly.

Combine hoisin sauce, ½ cup peanut oil and soy sauce in small bowl and blend well. Pour dressing over pork mixture and toss gently. Cover and refrigerate for up to 2 hours.

Meanwhile, pour peanut oil into large skillet to depth of ½ inch. Place over medium-high heat. When oil is hot, add 1 egg roll wrapper and fry until golden brown on both sides. Drain on paper towels. Repeat with remaining egg roll wrappers. Set aside.

To serve, arrange egg roll wrappers on 6 individual plates. Toss salad gently to reblend. Spoon salad over egg roll wrappers, dividing evenly.

6 ❦ Fruit Salads

It is really no surprise why artists through the centuries have chosen to immortalize the classic still life of fresh fruit: Few foods are as beautiful in their natural form—the pleasing shape of a ripe strawberry or the symmetry of a perfect pear. Yet fruits are perhaps the ultimate medium for culinary artistry as well. Always cool and refreshing, while at the same time satisfying and healthful, fruits, and fruit salads in particular, add an elegant, fresh-tasting note to any meal.

Fruit salads offer all kinds of advantages, not the least of which is adaptability. Many of the combinations in this chapter can lead a double life as appetizers or dessert. The Minted Grapes in Melon Halves (page 106), for instance, are an excellent first course when served with cheese breadsticks or warmed corn muffins, but they are also an excellent dessert on their own. Liqueur-Marinated Blueberries and Strawberries (page 105) are a colorful dessert for spring or summer, but they could also be a delightful side dish for brunch or lunch. Or, spoon them over pound cake or ice cream with afternoon tea.

Fruit salads also present some delectable contrasts in flavor and texture. Avocado and grapefruit may be traditional salad ingredients, but when dressed with a zesty blend of chili sauce, cider vinegar and sugar, they take on a delightful new character. Fresh Fruit with Lemon Curd (page 108) is simplicity itself. Prepare the tangy lemon mixture ahead and ready the fruit in easy stages, and you have an ideal centerpiece for your next party buffet. If the occasion calls for something a bit more exotic, Sweet Fruit with Coconut Sauce (page 108) fits the menu perfectly as a side dish for grilled pork or chicken, or simply for dessert. Curry and applesauce are an unlikely pair, but they create a marvelous topping for fruit. Or, omit the curry and try the blend on pancakes or crepes.

Always try to buy fruit in season if possible—flavor will be at its peak, and it is less expensive; for best results, leave any bruised or misshapen fruit in the produce bin at the market. And when creating one of the fresh fruit arrangements, think about color balance as well as texture and taste. No matter what you choose to make, you will be amply rewarded with a fresh, natural flavor that complements a wide range of menus.

Avocado and Grapefruit Salad

8 servings

4 ripe avocados
4 pink grapefruit
Romaine lettuce

Delicado Dressing (see following recipe)

Salt
Coarse cracked pepper

Peel and slice avocados. Peel grapefruit and separate sections. Make a bed of lettuce on a large serving platter. Alternate slices of avocado and grapefruit. Pour on Delicado Dressing. Season with salt and pepper. If you desire, you may prepare individual salad plates using ½ avocado and ½ grapefruit for each person.

Delicado Dressing

Makes about 1½ cups

2 tablespoons catsup or chili sauce
1 cup salad oil

¼ cup apple cider vinegar
1 tablespoon sugar

Combine all ingredients in a jar and shake well. Store in refrigerator. Just before serving, shake well again.

Avocado and Papaya Salad with Walnuts

4 servings

2 ripe avocados
3 tablespoons fresh lime juice
1 ripe papaya, peeled, seeded and sliced

1 tablespoon balsamico vinegar, red wine vinegar or Sherry vinegar

Salt and freshly ground pepper
½ cup walnut oil
½ cup coarsely chopped walnuts
Watercress sprigs (garnish)

Peel, halve and pit avocados. Place cut side down on chilled plate and rub with some of lime juice. Arrange papaya slices like fan on plate. Slice and fan avocado in the same way.

Combine remaining lime juice with vinegar, salt and pepper in mixing bowl and stir until salt dissolves. Beat in oil. Add walnuts and let stand about a minute. Remove and sprinkle over avocado and papaya. Dip watercress in dressing; remove. Pour dressing over fruit and garnish with watercress.

Avocado Fruit Delight

4 servings

Juice of 1 lime
2 ripe avocados, peeled, pitted and cut into bite-size chunks
2 ripe bananas, sliced
1 apple, chopped into bite-size chunks

½ cup shredded unsweetened coconut
¼ cup dates, chopped
½ cup walnuts, chopped

Sprinkle lime juice over avocado chunks. Mix avocados with all remaining ingredients except walnuts. Toss. Serve topped with walnuts.

🍎 *The Care and Selection of Berries*

Remember that big is not necessarily best: Sometimes the smaller berry can be more flavorful.

Be wary of cartons stained with juice, a sign that the contents may be overripe or crushed. After you bring the berries home, transfer them to a bowl as soon as possible and discard the bruised or mildewed ones. Then cover and refrigerate, unwashed and unhulled.

With the exception of the fragile raspberry, too delicate to withstand rinsing, berries should be washed just before use.

Sugar blueberries just before serving; strawberries one hour in advance; boysenberries and blackberries—usually sold somewhat underripe—two to three hours ahead. (Longer maceration allows them to develop full flavor.)

Liqueur-Marinated Blueberries and Strawberries

This also makes an excellent dessert.

8 servings

2 cups fresh blueberries
1 pint fresh strawberries

¼ cup orange liqueur

Combine berries in bowl and pour liqueur over. Cover and refrigerate several hours. Spoon berries and some liqueur into clear glass or crystal compotes, wine glasses or goblets.

Cranberry Salad

10 to 12 servings

2 3-ounce packages cream cheese, room temperature
2 tablespoons mayonnaise
2 tablespoons sugar
1 16-ounce can cranberry sauce, whole berry style

1 11-ounce can mandarin oranges, drained
½ cup chopped walnuts, lightly toasted
1 cup whipping cream, whipped

Grease 1½-quart plain ring mold. Line with plastic wrap or aluminum foil, overlapping edges by at least 1 inch.

Beat cream cheese with mayonnaise and sugar until smooth. Gently blend in cranberry sauce, oranges and walnuts, using wooden spoon. Fold in whipped cream. Pour into mold. Freeze at least 6 hours. Unmold onto platter.

🍎

Cranberry-Citrus Salad

8 servings

Escarole, Boston and romaine lettuce, washed and chilled
2 8-ounce cans chilled cranberry sauce, whole berry style
1 8-ounce can grapefruit sections, chilled and drained
1 8-ounce can orange sections, chilled and drained

Pomegranate seeds (optional)
Sweet-Sour Dressing (see following recipe)

Line a large platter with lettuce leaves. Slice contents of chilled cans of cranberry sauce into four rounds each. Put cranberry slices, grapefruit and orange sections on lettuce. Sprinkle with pomegranate seeds. Serve with Sweet-Sour Dressing.

Sweet-Sour Dressing

Makes ½ cup

½ cup mayonnaise
1 tablespoon honey

2 teaspoons vinegar
¼ teaspoon celery seed

Combine all ingredients and refrigerate until ready to use. This dressing is best if made ahead.

Endive and Grapefruit Salad

8 servings

6 Belgian endive

3 pink grapefruit

6 tablespoons walnut oil
1 teaspoon fresh lemon juice

¾ teaspoon Dijon mustard
¼ teaspoon salt
Freshly ground white pepper

8 watercress sprigs (garnish)

Cut stem ends from endive and discard. Remove 24 of the largest outer leaves and set aside *(be careful not to tear leaves)*. Cut remaining endive crosswise into ½-inch pieces and transfer to large bowl.

Hold 1 grapefruit over another bowl to catch juice and, using sharp knife, peel grapefruit to remove both outer peel and inner white pith. Cut along membrane and carefully remove segments, then cut into ½-inch pieces. Add to endive. Repeat with remaining grapefruit. Toss lightly. Cover and chill.

Measure 3 tablespoons of the grapefruit juice into small jar. Add oil, lemon juice, mustard, salt and pepper. Cover tightly and shake vigorously until well blended. Taste and adjust seasoning with lemon juice, mustard or salt.

Arrange 3 reserved endive leaves in fan pattern on each of 8 salad plates, with flat ends meeting at center. Mound some of grapefruit mixture over top. Drizzle each with 1 tablespoon dressing and garnish with watercress sprig.

Minted Grapes in Melon Halves

Serve with cheese bread sticks or warmed corn muffins.

4 servings

4 cups seedless grapes (or halved and seeded grapes)
1 tablespoon minced fresh mint
1 cup yogurt
2 tablespoons honey

½ teaspoon grated ginger
2 medium melons (not watermelon), halved, seeded, room temperature

Toss grapes with mint; chill well. Mix together yogurt, honey and ginger in blender and fold into grapes. Heap grape mixture into melon halves.

Amaretto Oranges with Ricotta and Strawberries

4 servings

2 large navel oranges, peeled and sliced into thin rings
2 tablespoons amaretto liqueur
½ pound ricotta cheese, drained and pureed
3 tablespoons chopped toasted almonds

2 tablespoons sugar
2 tablespoons chopped candied fruit
½ teaspoon vanilla
12 strawberries, hulled
12 fresh mint leaves (garnish)

Place sliced oranges in storage container and sprinkle with liqueur. Cover and refrigerate overnight.

Combine cheese, almonds, sugar, fruit and vanilla in medium mixing bowl. Shape into 16 small balls. Arrange in container with tight-fitting lid. Cover and refrigerate overnight.

To serve, arrange oranges in overlapping pattern on 4 dessert plates. Set 4 cheese balls on each plate. Place 3 strawberries next to cheese, slipping mint leaves under berries for garnish.

Assorted Fruits with Almond Balls

12 to 16 servings

Fruits (use any of the following to total 4 to 6 cups)
    Lichees
    Loquats
    Mandarin orange sections
    Longans
    Cantaloupe balls
    Watermelon balls
    Apricots, peeled and halved or quartered
    Peaches, peeled and halved or quartered
    Plums, peeled and halved or quartered

    Seedless grapes
    Pineapple chunks marinated in Triple Sec
    Strawberries marinated in kirsch

Almond Balls
1½ cups whole almonds, toasted
1¼ cups powdered sugar
  1 egg white
1½ teaspoons almond extract
 ⅛ teaspoon (heaping) salt

For fruits: Combine as desired; chill.

For almond balls: Grind almonds in processor or blender. Add remaining ingredients and mix to a stiff paste. Form into balls ½ inch in diameter. Arrange on platter. Cover loosely and refrigerate overnight. Just before serving, mound fruit in center of platter.

Don's Pomeroy House Salad

6 to 8 servings

1 head lettuce, torn into small pieces
2 bunches spinach (12 ounces total), washed, drained and stemmed
1 small head red cabbage (4 ounces), finely shredded
1 12-ounce can mandarin oranges, drained

12 strawberries, hulled and quartered
½ Bermuda onion, sliced into ¼-inch rings
Honey–poppy seed dressing or vinaigrette (use your favorite recipe)

Combine lettuce, spinach and cabbage in large salad bowl. Arrange oranges along inside rim of bowl. Top oranges with berries. Cover salad with Bermuda onion. Top with dressing. Cover and refrigerate. Toss salad at table when ready to serve.

Fresh Fruit with Lemon Curd

Makes 6 cups

16 egg yolks
2 cups sugar
1½ cups fresh lemon juice
Coarsely grated or chopped peel of 2 lemons
1½ cups (3 sticks) unsalted butter, melted

2 cups whipping cream
Fresh fruit (strawberries, kiwi, grapes, honeydew or other melon, Pippin or Granny Smith apples, etc.)
Grated lemon peel

Combine yolks, sugar, lemon juice and peel in top of double boiler set over simmering water and whisk until light and fluffy. Remove from heat and whisk in butter 1 tablespoon at a time. Cool.

Beat whipping cream in medium bowl until soft peaks form. Gently fold into lemon curd. To serve, spoon over fresh fruit and sprinkle with additional grated lemon peel.

Buah Kuah Ketan Sirkaya
(Sweet Fruit with Coconut Sauce)

Serves 6

Fruits (use any of the following to total 3 cups)
  Apples, peeled and cored, cut into 8 slices
  Pears, cored and cut into 8 slices
  Pineapple, peeled and cut into 1-inch wedges
  Bananas, cut into ¾-inch diagonal slices
  Melon, peeled, cut into 1-inch wedges
  Papaya, peeled and seeded, cut into 1-inch wedges

  Mango, peeled and seeded, cut into slices
  Kiwi fruit, peeled, sliced

1½ cups coconut milk
2 well-beaten eggs
5 tablespoons dark brown sugar
2 teaspoons lemon peel, grated
2 tablespoons coconut liqueur or 1 teaspoon coconut extract plus 1½ tablespoons Cognac
2 tablespoons Cognac

Place fruits of your choice in a large glass bowl or on a large platter.

In top of a double boiler, combine coconut milk, eggs and brown sugar. Mix thoroughly and add lemon peel. Stirring continuously, simmer over hot water until sauce thickens. Remove from heat and add coconut liqueur and Cognac. Pour over fruit. Using your hands, mix very gently, being careful not to crush or break the fruit.

Les Trois Fruits

10 to 12 servings

Bananas
- 6 bananas, quartered and cut into 2-inch pieces
- 1/3 cup sugar
- Juice of 1 lime
- Peel of 1 lime, cut into 1/4-inch pieces
- Juice of 1/2 lemon
- Peel of 1/2 lemon, cut into 1/4-inch pieces

Combine all ingredients in serving dish (preferably clear glass) and toss lightly. Cover and chill several hours.

Prunes*
- 3 cups water
- 1 cup sugar
- 2 tablespoons minced fresh cilantro
- 2 tablespoons Armagnac, Cognac or orange liqueur
- 1 tablespoon whole black peppercorns tied in cheesecloth
- 1 pound dried pitted prunes

Combine all ingredients except prunes in large saucepan and simmer 15 minutes, stirring until sugar is dissolved. Remove peppercorns. Add fruit and poach 10 minutes. Cool in syrup. Serve at room temperature or chilled.

Figs
- 1 1/2 cups water
- 1/2 cup cassis syrup or liqueur
- 1/2 cup sugar
- 2 tablespoons diced unpeeled lemon
- 12 fresh figs, peeled

Combine all ingredients except figs in medium saucepan and simmer 10 minutes. Add figs and poach gently 3 minutes. Cool in syrup. Serve either at room temperature or chilled.

*Six peeled fresh pears or 12 peeled fresh plums may be substituted for prunes.

Winter Fruit Salad

4 servings

- 2 firm medium apples, cored and cubed
- 2 bananas, halved lengthwise, cut into 1-inch pieces
- 8 dried apricots or 4 dried peach or nectarine halves, coarsely chopped
- 4 dried pitted prunes, coarsely chopped
- 1/2 cup raisins
- 3 to 5 heaping tablespoons plain yogurt
- 1/2 tablespoon honey
- Dash of nutmeg
- 1 to 2 tablespoons orange or apple juice or Grand Marnier
- 2 tablespoons coarsely chopped toasted almonds

Combine first 8 ingredients in medium bowl and mix well. Stir in juice or liqueur to taste. Cover and chill. When ready to serve, gently mix in almonds.

Fresh Fruit Fantasy

For this edible centerpiece, use any fruits that are in season. Wherever possible, cut into sections or quarters. This recipe is only one combination you might try.

Serves 12

Evergreen branches or ivy
4 large bunches seedless grapes
6 tangerines, quartered with skin folded back
1 ripe papaya, quartered and left unseeded (the dark, edible seeds provide contrast)
1 honeydew melon, cut into wedges and seeded
4 small pears, left whole

Spread branches in shallow basket. Fill with fruits in an informal arrangement. Cover lightly with plastic wrap and chill or keep cool. Just before serving, sprinkle lightly with a bit of water for added sheen. Make sure everyone has both knife and fork. Surround with breads, cheeses, jams and butter.

Orange Salad with Rose Water

This Moroccan salad can be served as a first course or a refreshing dessert.

12 servings

6 navel oranges, peeled and sliced into circles
2 tablespoons powdered sugar
1½ teaspoons rose water
2 generous pinches cinnamon

Arrange orange slices in overlapping pattern in serving dish. Sprinkle with remaining ingredients, cover and chill before serving.

Cold Fruit Bowl

8 servings

1 15-ounce can loquats, undrained
1 11-ounce can mandarin oranges, drained
1 11-ounce can lichee nuts, drained
1 8-ounce can pineapple chunks, drained, or about ¼ fresh pineapple, cubed
1 8-ounce jar preserved kumquats, drained
1 pint strawberries, halved
Preserved ginger (optional)

Combine fruits with syrup from loquats. Top with shredded ginger, if desired. Serve chilled or at room temperature.

Cool Fruit Salad

4 servings

1 cup plain yogurt
1 tablespoon honey
1 teaspoon vanilla or almond extract
½ teaspoon cinnamon
Pinch of nutmeg
Assorted freshly cut fruit (apples, bananas, pineapple, peaches, strawberries, grapes)
Shredded coconut (garnish)

Combine first 5 ingredients in small bowl and mix well. Arrange fruit in individual serving dishes. Spoon some of sauce over top. Garnish with coconut.

Vermont Fruit Salad

8 to 10 servings

2 cups plain yogurt
3 tablespoons maple syrup
½ teaspoon cinnamon
1 pound trail mix
3 large navel oranges, peeled and separated into sections

3 large bananas, peeled and sliced into ¼-inch rounds
3 large firm pears, quartered, cored and sliced
2 pink grapefruit, peeled and separated into sections

Mix first 3 ingredients in small bowl. Combine remaining ingredients in large serving bowl. Pour sauce over and toss lightly. Cover and chill at least 4 hours. Toss again before serving.

Fruit and Yogurt Bowl

This is good with honey muffins for lunch or with baked fish and steamed vegetables for dinner.

4 main-course, or 5 to 6 side-dish servings

1 medium cantaloupe, cut into 1-inch pieces
3 cups strawberries, hulled
3 peaches, sliced
2 large bananas, sliced
1 cup seedless grapes
½ cup unsweetened shredded coconut

2 cups yogurt
3 to 4 tablespoons honey
2 teaspoons vanilla
Lettuce leaves
Chopped nuts or sunflower seeds (optional garnish)

Lightly combine fruits with coconut. Mix yogurt, honey and vanilla in blender. Fold into fruit mixture. Chill. Serve on lettuce leaves. Garnish with nuts or seeds, if desired.

Fruit Salad

This healthy combination is a colorful dessert presentation for brunch or a light supper. Peel oranges, limes and pineapple over a bowl to catch the juices, which will be used to thin the mayonnaise for the dressing.

8 servings

1 head curly endive or chicory
4 oranges, peeled and thinly sliced
4 bananas, thinly sliced
1 jicama, peeled, halved lengthwise and thinly sliced
3 limes, peeled and thinly sliced

1 small pineapple, peeled, cored and thinly sliced into rings

4 red apples, unpeeled, cored and thinly sliced into rings
8 cooked small beets, peeled and very thinly sliced
1 or 2 Orange and Poppy Seed Yogurt Cheese Rounds (see following recipe)

1 cup mayonnaise

Separate endive or chicory leaves. Line sides of large shallow serving bowl with the most attractive leaves. Shred remainder and sprinkle over bottom of bowl. Alternate overlapping slices of orange and banana around edge of bowl, reserving any extra orange slices. Arrange jicama slices in circle next to oranges. Place lime slices on jicama.

Alternate overlapping slices of pineapple and apple inside circle, adding any remaining orange slices. Bend and overlap beet slices to resemble flower petals and place in center. Break off small pieces of yogurt cheese round(s) and roll into small balls. Sprinkle over salad or mound in center of beets.

Thin mayonnaise to desired consistency with reserved fruit juices. Spoon over salad or pass separately.

Orange and Poppyseed Yogurt Cheese Rounds

Makes 5 rounds (about ⅔ cup each)

4 cups good quality plain yogurt (homemade or commercial)

2 cups large curd creamed cottage cheese

3 tablespoons freshly squeezed orange juice

1 tablespoon finely chopped orange peel

1 tablespoon honey

Poppy seed (garnish)

Spread 2 layers of dampened cheesecloth in large bowl. Pour yogurt into cheesecloth. Pull the four corners of cheesecloth together and tie securely (kitchen sink is a convenient place for draining; tie bag to faucet). Repeat with cottage cheese. Let stand until yogurt and cottage cheese are completely drained and firm, about 10 to 12 hours or overnight. (Time will vary depending on moisture content.)

Preheat oven to 225°F. Lightly oil 5 deep 1-cup ovenproof dishes. Carefully remove cheesecloth and transfer drained yogurt and cottage cheese to large bowl (there should be approximately 2 cups drained yogurt and 1½ cups drained cottage cheese). Mix together gently, adding orange juice, orange peel and honey. Divide among prepared dishes, pressing into small rounds. Bake 1½ hours. Turn rounds over in cups and continue baking until dry and firm, about 1½ hours. Let cool completely before transferring to wire rack. Garnish with generous sprinkling of poppy seed.

Fresh Fruit Fantasia

Can be topped with raspberry ice or cottage cheese and served surrounded with banana bread sandwiches, grapes and parsley for garnish.

1 serving

1 large cup-shaped iceberg lettuce leaf

2 sections grapefruit

2 slices cantaloupe

2 slices honeydew

1 slice orange

2 slices pineapple

2 cubes watermelon (or a few slices of plum, nectarine or peach)

3 fresh strawberries or cherries

Poppy Seed Dressing (see following recipe)

Strawberries (garnish)

Wash and dry lettuce leaf and tear in half lengthwise. Put the halves inside each other to form a cup.

Peel fruit. Place fruit into lettuce cup in order listed, starting with grapefruit and ending with 3 strawberries.

Top with Poppy Seed Dressing and garnish with strawberries.

Poppy Seed Dressing

1½ cups sugar

2 teaspoons dry mustard

2 teaspoons salt

⅔ cup vinegar

3 tablespoons onion juice*

2 cups salad oil

3 tablespoons poppy seed

Mix together sugar, mustard, salt and vinegar in blender. Add onion juice and blend thoroughly. With blender running, add oil slowly and continue blending until thick. Add poppy seed and whirl for a few more seconds. Store covered in a cool place or keep in the refrigerator.

*Make onion juice by grating a large white onion on the fine side of a grater or by chopping it in blender, then straining.

Tossed Fruit Salad

8 servings

Dressing

1 cup safflower oil
⅓ cup white vinegar
¼ cup sugar or to taste
1 tablespoon poppy seed (optional)
1 teaspoon dry mustard
1 teaspoon salt

Salad

2 heads lettuce, washed, dried and torn into bite-size pieces
1 pint fresh strawberries (if available), hulled and halved
2 oranges, peeled and diced
2 avocados, peeled and diced

For dressing: Combine first 6 ingredients in blender and mix until thickened. Chill well.

For salad: Combine ingredients except avocado in salad bowl. Cover and chill. Add avocado just before ready to serve.

To serve, pour dressing over salad and toss to coat.

Apple Dressing

A refreshing topping for fruit.

Makes about 2 cups

1 cup smooth, thick applesauce
½ cup plain yogurt
½ cup sour cream

2 tablespoons fresh lemon or lime juice
Curry powder

Blend applesauce, yogurt, sour cream and lemon juice until smooth. Thin with a little water if necessary. Add curry powder to taste and blend well.

🍎 Index

🍎 Credits and Acknowledgments

The following people contributed the recipes included in this book:
Judith Adams
Paul Bocuse
Patricia Brooks
Sandra Brown
Audrey Buckle
Sharon Cadwallader
Anna Teresa Callen
Duane Cerney
Cecilia Chiang
Mary Beth Clark
Claudette Cole
Charlotte Combe
Cooper's Seafood House, Scranton, Pennsylvania
Dinah Corley
Terri D'Ancona
Narsai David
Suzanne Delaney
Phyllis Diller
Diane Dodd-MacKenzie
Daphne Doerr
Don's Pomeroy House, Strongsville, Ohio
Alain Dutournier
Inger Elliott
Helen Feingold
Barbara Feldstein
Chuck Flannery-Jones
Fo-Fo-Th-Bo, Hendersonville, North Carolina
Karalee Fox
Phyllis Fox-Krupp
Jany Gade
Edith Gaines
Julie Gordon
Marion Gorman
Freddi Greenberg
Hastings House, Salt Spring Island, Canada
Elaine Hill
Jacquolene Young Hursey
Elizabeth James
John Nero Restaurant, Greenbay, Wisconsin
Barbara Karoff
Lynne Kasper
Saralee Kucera
Dona Kuryanowicz
Alma Lach
Rita Leinwand
Le Pavillon, Vancouver, Canada
The Magnolia Hotel, Yountville, California, Owners Bruce and Bonnie Locken

Ma Maison, Los Angeles, California
Abby Mandel
Amy C. Marchand
Copeland Marks
Norma Matlin
Joel McCormick III
Perla Meyers
Iris and Allen Mink
Jeanne Moreau
Jinx and Jefferson Morgan
Neiman-Marcus, Northbrook, Illinois
Judith N. Olert
Judith Olney
Daniel Pannebaker
Margaret Prochaska
The Prospect of Westport, Kansas City, Missouri
Joanna Pruess
Wolfgang Puck
The Quilted Giraffe, New York, New York, Barry Wine
Rosa Rajković
Theo Ravin
Frans Reyer
Jill Roberts
Nell Rugee
Sondra Rykoff
Rosalie Saferstein
Susan Sandler
Shirley Sarvis
Eleanor Schultz
Jan Shannon
Edena Sheldon
Shun Lee Palace, New York, New York
Elsie Silva
Cornelia and Mike Smollin
Stox II, Buena Park, California
Barbara Tomorowitz
Jeremiah Tower
May Wong Trent
Trianon Continental Restaurant, Portland, Oregon, Chef Otto Fennerl
Michele Urvater
Jan Weimer
Robert Weiss
Marty Westerman
Anne Willan
Gina Wilson
Paula Wolfert

Additional text was supplied by:
Lynne Kasper, *How to Buy and Use Olive Oil*
Rita Leinwand, *Brown Stocks, Salad, Sauce Vinaigrette, Classic Mayonnaise*

Perla Meyers, *The Care and Selection of Berries*
Jan Weimer, *Vegetable Soups, Fish Stock*

Special thanks to:
Marilou Vaughan, *Editor, Bon Appétit*
Barbara Varnum,
    Associate Editor, Bon Appétit
Bernard Rotondo,
    Art Director, Bon Appétit
Leslie A. Dame,
    Editorial Assistant, Bon Appétit
Anthony P. Iacono,
    Vice-President Manufacturing, Knapp Communications Corporation
Philip Kaplan, *Vice-President, Executive Graphics, Knapp Communications Corporation*
Patrick R. Casey,
    Vice-President, Production, Knapp Communications Corporation
G. Dean Larrabee and Karen Legier,
    Rights and Permissions Coordinators, Knapp Communications Corporation
Diana Rico
Elaine Linden
June Gader
Sonsie Conroy

The Knapp Press
is a wholly owned subsidary of
KNAPP COMMUNICATIONS CORPORATION
Chairman and Chief Executive Officer:
    Cleon T. Knapp
President: H. Stephen Cranston
Senior Vice-Presidents:
    Paige Rense (*Editor-in-Chief*)
    Everett T. Alcan (*Corporate Planning*)
    Rosalie Bruno (*New Venture Development*)
    John L. Decker (*Magazine Group Publisher*)
    Betsy Wood Knapp (*MIS Electronic Media*)
    L. James Wade, Jr. (*Finance*)

THE KNAPP PRESS
President: Alice Bandy; *Administrative Assistant:* Beth Bell; *Senior Editor:* Norman Kolpas; *Associate Editors:* Jeff Book, Jan Koot, Sarah Lifton, Pamela Mosher; *Assistant Editor:* Taryn Bigelow; *Editorial Coordinator:* Jan Stuebing; *Editorial Assistant:* Nancy D. Roberts; *Art Director:* Paula Schlosser; *Design Associates:* Robin Murawski, Nan Oshin; *Production Manager:* Larry Cooke; *Production Coordinator:* Joan Valentine; *Financial Manager:* Robert Groag; *Financial Analyst:* Carlton Joseph; *Financial Assistant:* Kerri Culbertson; *Fulfillment Services Manager:* Virginia Parry; *Marketing Manager:* Jan B. Fox; *Promotions Manager:* Jeanie Gould; *Marketing Assistants:* Dolores Briqueleur, Joanne Denison; *Special Sales:* Lynn Blocker; *Department Secretaries:* Amy Hershman, Randy Levin

This book is set in Sabon, a face designed by Jan Teischold in 1967 and based on early fonts engraved by Garamond and Granjon.

Composition was on the Mergenthaler Linotron 202 by Graphic Typesetting Service.

Series design by Paula Schlosser. Page layout by Nan Oshin.

Text stock: Allied Superior A.F. Offset, Basis 65. Color plate stock: Mead Northcote Basis 70. Both furnished by WWF Paper Corporation West.

Color separations by NEC Incorporated.

Printing and binding by R.R. Donnelley and Sons.